Parlez-Vous Frenglish?

Countless apt locutions from French have entered the English language, some becoming everyday phrases, others tossed around recklessly by film critics and gourmets. Until now there hasn't been a single handy source a non-French speaker could turn to for explanation—or *riposte*.

Je Ne Sais What?, with *beaucoup de définitions* of commonly used phrases and names, is the perfect browsing antidote to *ennui*, the perfect gift for Francophiles, armchair linguists, and crossword addicts. And for those who want to understand French phrases in pretentious movie reviews, or dazzle their friends at dinner parties, this delightful guide is certain to be a *succès fou* (smash hit). *Voilà*!

JON WINOKUR is the bestselling author of *The Portable Curmudgeon* and various other books. He lives in Pacific Palisades, California.

Also by Jon Winokur

Fathers
The Portable Curmudgeon Redux
True Confessions
Mondo Canine
Friendly Advice
A Curmudgeon's Garden of Love
Zen to Go
The Portable Curmudgeon
Writers on Writing

Je Ne Sais What?

A Guide to *de rigueur* Frenglish for Readers, Writers, and Speakers

~

Jon Winokur

Illustrations by William Bramhall

A PLUME BOOK

PLUME
Published by the Penguin Group
Penguin Books USA Inc., 375 Hudson Street,
New York, New York 10014, U.S.A.
Penguin Books Ltd, 27 Wrights Lane, London W8 5TZ, England
Penguin Books Australia Ltd, Ringwood, Victoria, Australia
Penguin Books Canada Ltd, 10 Alcorn Avenue, Toronto, Ontario, Canada M4V 3B2
Penguin Books (N.Z.) Ltd, 182–190 Wairau Road, Auckland 10, New Zealand

Penguin Books Ltd, Registered Offices: Harmondsworth, Middlesex, England

Published by Plume, an imprint of Dutton Signet,
a division of Penguin Books USA Inc.
Previously published in a Dutton edition.

First Plume Printing, November, 1996
10 9 8 7 6 5 4 3 2 1

"Down with *Englench!*" by Ellen Goodman © 1993, the *Washington Post* Writer's
Group. Reprinted with permission.

 REGISTERED TRADEMARK—MARCA REGISTRADA

The Library of Congress has catalogued the Dutton edition as follows:
Winokur, Jon.
    Je ne sais what? : a guide to de rigueur Frenglish for readers,
writers, and speakers / Jon Winokur ; illustrations by William
Bramhall.
        p.   cm.
    ISBN 0-525-93703-X (hc.)
    ISBN 0-452-27200-9 (pbk.)
    1. English language—Foreign words and phrases—French—
Glossaries, vocabularies, etc.   2. French language—Influence on
English—Glossaries, vocabularies, etc.   I. Title.
PE1582.F8W56   1995
422'.441—dc20   94–34673
                                                            CIP

Printed in the United States of America
Original hardcover design by Leonard Telesca

To Mark Wolgin, *bon copain*

Acknowledgments

I wish to thank Peter Bell and Michael Wolgin for their wise counsel, Hugh Rawson for an expert opinion, Professor Murray Sachs of Brandeis University for felicitous and erudite comments and suggestions, and Eugene Ehrlich, whose *Amo, Amas, Amat, and More* is the paradigm for this book. I'm especially indebted to Reid Boates, *honnête homme*; Norrie Epstein, for countless sparkling *aperçus*; Margo Kaufman, for a *coup de maître*; Rachel Klayman, *femme savante*; and, as always, Elinor Winokur, *grande dame*.

Contents

Introduction

This book is intended as a quick reference to the definitions, pronunciation, and origins of "Frenglish," those ubiquitous French expressions, maxims, literary allusions, and terms of art that grace English discourse. It is also meant to be a good browse, illuminating such delectable Gallicisms as *je ne sais quoi, c'est la vie, joie de vivre, entre nous, fait accompli*, and *de rigueur*. It likewise celebrates French terms used less frequently in English but valuable nonetheless for their expressiveness and charm (*esprit de l'escalier*, for example, literally "staircase wit," a clever remark thought of too late).

The main body of the book consists of an alphabetical listing of Frenglish words and phrases with definitions, and, in many cases, brief etymological notes and illustrative quotations. In most entries the literal meaning of the word or phrase is given first, followed by the idiomatic definition(s). I've employed a simplified pronunciation guide, which I considered preferable to a system involving arcane phonetic symbols. And the compilation is not exhaustive: I haven't tried to include every key word or phrase in the ever-expanding Frenglish lexicon—the task is too great and the choice too subjective.

Unlike Franglais, which is a hybrid of French and English, Frenglish is pure, grammatically correct French. But Frenglish and French aren't necessarily identical. Some Frenglish words are no longer used by French speakers, while others have different meanings than in the original French. Thus the terms *objet de vertu, bon viveur, cul-de-sac*, and *blanc-mange*, among others, have different meanings for Francophones. An American might say *savoir-faire* to express what a Frenchman would call *le know-how*, and while *raconteur* connotes wit and sophistication for us, the French associate it with someone who tells long, boring stories.

A few Frenglish words have made reverse migrations, having returned to France from America after acquiring a layer of meaning here, thereby completing a round-trip. *Pedigree*, for example, from the French *pié de grue* ("crane's foot"), a term describing the symbol originally used as an abbreviation for "begat" ("Alphonse and Françoise > Pierre"), was adopted as *pedigree* in English and has returned to French as an "Americanism." Other words that have made reverse migrations include *vaudeville* (named after a town in Normandy) and *apache*, a Parisian street ruffian or thug, and also a dance in which the male simulates rough treatment of his female partner (and hence any man who abuses women), originally named after the tribe of American Indians.

It is difficult to overstate the impact of French on English. Much of our political, military, artistic, and culinary vocabulary originated in France. While English has become the international language of science and technology, French is still the *nonpareil* for apt expression, the linguistic *sauce piquante* of Western civilization. Countless elegant Gallicisms infuse American English. And the British are even more receptive: They use more French words and phrases than we do, and they pronounce them better. But then, we Americans take perverse pride in our inability to speak foreign languages.

Although it has steadily lost international influence since World War I, French hasn't lost its cachet. It's still the natural language of love, fashion, cooking, and diplomacy. It's still elegant and precise, an *adult* language, ideal for expressing urbane thoughts and worldly wisdom. It clears the cognitive palate: Whenever I come upon a bit of felicitous Frenglish in a book or magazine article, I'm instantly transported to a café in Paris. For a split-second, "La vie en rose" plays in the background, I smell Gauloises and taste Pernod. Frenglish is an exotic treat, an evanescent literary pleasure, delightfully different from English. *Vive la différence!*

J. W.
Pacific Palisades, California
September 1994

Pronunciation

~

French pronunciation is quirky, with many sounds that don't exist in English. "Nasalized vowels," for example: The French *grand*, though spelled the same as its English cognate, is pronounced as if the speaker has a deviated septum. Likewise *bon*, pronounced not as "bahn" or "bone," but something like "bawn." And the *in* in *au gratin* sounds vaguely like the noise made by sheep.

The French uvular *r* (*crêpe, roué*) is even more extreme, uttered as if the speaker with the deviated septum is also clearing his throat. And then there's the *u* in *plus, luxe*, and *légume*, similar to the umlauted *u* in German. To pronounce it, start to say "oo," but then purse the lips to make it "ee." Pronounce the *j* in *jour* approximately like the second *g* in garage, and for the *eu* in *deux* or *bleu*, don't say "dew" or "blew," say "duh" and "bluh."

In *intime*, the first *i* is pronounced something like the *o* in "on," the second like the *e* in "me." The acute-accented *e* is pronounced either as "eh" or "ay," depending on where it occurs. To the anglophone ear, *droit* sounds almost like "dwah," and *tableau* like "tab low" (but don't bet the *château* on it), and the *aise* in *Française* rhymes with Pez.

Given these nuances, a comprehensive pronunciation guide would require the reader to thumb back and forth between entries and a long list of exotic phonetic symbols. Since the focus of this book is on written rather than spoken French, and in the interest of utility, I've opted for this simplified pronunciation key:

GUIDE SYMBOL	FRENCH	ENGLISH
a^n	*grand, sans, amant*	quantity
o^n	*bon, cordon*	long, laundry
ü	*légume, humaine*	[like the English sound "ee," with the lips in a tight circle]
zh	*jour, agent, voyage*	vision, garage

All other phonetic translations are pronounced as in English. Stress is indicated by boldface type.

Boy, those French, they have a different word for everything!
—STEVE MARTIN

a

à bas (ah **bah**) down with; off with.

abattoir (ah bah **twahr**) a slaughterhouse (from *abattre*, "to strike down").

abbé (ah **bay**) abbot; priest.

abbé de cour (ah **bay** duh **koor**) court priest; a worldly cleric.

à bientôt (ah bye^n **toh**) so long; see you soon.

à bon appétit il ne faut point de sauce (ah bo^n nah pay tee eel nuh **foh** pwa^n duh **sohs**) A good appetite needs no sauce.

à bon chat, bon rat (ah bo^n **shah**, bo^n **rah**) "To a good cat, a good rat"; tit for tat.

à bon droit (ah bo^n **drwah**) with good reason; justly. Synonymous with *à bonne raison*.

à bon marché (ah bo^n mahr **shay**) at a good bargain; cheap.

à bonne raison (ah **bun** reh **zo**^{n}) with good reason; justly; synonymous with *à bon droit*.

à bras ouverts (ah **brahz** oo **vehr**) with open arms; cordially.

absinthe (ahb **sa**^{n}t) a strong liqueur made from an aromatic herb, *artemisia absinthium*, also called common wormwood. The pale green, anise-flavored drink was served by pouring it over a lump of sugar on a perforated spoon balanced on the lip of a glass. It was so popular in the cafés of Paris at the end of the nineteenth century that the late afternoon was known as *l'heure verte* (the "green hour"). *Absinthe* was a favorite of writers and artists, who called it the Green Fairy and the Green Muse. Degas, Manet, Toulouse-Lautrec, Van Gogh, and Picasso painted it; Verlaine, Rimbaud, Poe, Wilde, and Hemingway wrote about it. Unfortunately, it turned out to be an extremely toxic, sometimes lethal drug, and it was banned in 1915.

> Some of our bohemian poets have called *absinthe* the green Muse. Some others, not in this group, have died from the poisonous embraces of this same Muse. Hégesippe Moreau, Amédée Roland and Alfred de Musset, our greatest poet after Hugo and Lamartine, all succumbed to the disastrous effects of this liqueur.
>
> The fatal passion of de Musset for absinthe, which perhaps served also to give his verses such a bitter flavor, caused the sober Academy to fall into the near likeness of a pun. The fact was that de Musset missed many sessions of the Academy, finding himself not in a fit state to attend.
>
> "In truth," said M. Villemain, one of the Forty, "Do you not find that Alfred de Musset is *absent* a little too frequently?"
>
> "You mean to say that he *absinths* himself too much."
>
> —ALEXANDRE DUMAS, père, *Grand Dictionnaire de Cuisine*

Académie Française (ah kah day **mee** frah^n **sez**) the forty-member French literary academy established by Cardinal Richelieu (1585–1642) in 1634 to uphold literary standards and defend the purity of the French language. Soon after its founding the Academy began compiling a dictionary of the French language, but some 350 years later the reference work is still unfinished (though much of it has been published). See also, (*les*) *Immortels*.

> The principal function of the academy shall be to labor with all care and diligence to give certain rules to our language, and to render it pure, eloquent, and capable of treating the arts and sciences.
>
> —STATUTES OF THE ACADÉMIE FRANÇAISE, 1635

accablé (ah kah **blay**) crushed; overwhelmed.

accouchement (ah koosh **mah**^{n}) "lying in"; childbirth. From the verb *accoucher*, "to assist during childbirth," *accouchement* is the Frenglish euphemism for parturition.

accueil (ah kuh y^e) reception; welcome; greeting; honoring (of bills).

à cheval (ah shuh **vahl**) "on horseback"; a line of troops extending along the sides of a stream or road; in roulette, a bet placed on the line between two numbers.

à compte (ah ko^{n}t) on account; in partial payment.

à contre coeur (ah ko^n truh **kuhr**) against one's better instincts or feelings; against the grain; reluctantly.

à corps perdu (ah **kohr** pehr **dü**) "with lost body"; headlong; impetuously.

à coup sûr (ah koo **sür**) "with sure stroke"; unerringly; without fail.

acte gratuit (**ahkt** grah **twee**) an impulsive, motiveless act. A term coined by André Gide as part of his doctrine of individualist morality, according to which it is necessary to yield to a desire (by committing an *acte gratuit*) in order to gain control over it.

> Times have changed since 1960, when Norman Mailer, in a flashy *acte gratuit*, stabbed his wife in the chest during a party.
>
> —RHODA KOENIG, *The Independent*

à demi (ah duh **mee**) half; by halves; half done; incomplete.

à deux (ah **duh**) "for two"; between two; two persons alone together.

adieu (ah **dyuh**) "to God"; farewell. *Adieu* has a distinct connotation of finality and is therefore not synonymous with *au revoir*.

> Since you are ready to take up reports, and to judge so rashly as you do, I cannot but conclude you are some peevish or melancholy man, not fit to be discoursed with; and so *adieu*.
>
> —JOHN BUNYAN, *The Pilgrim's Progress*

à droite (ah **drwaht**) on the right.

affaire d'amour (ah **fehr** dah **moor**) love affair.

affaire de coeur (ah **fehr** duh **kuhr**) "affair of the heart"; love affair.

affaire d'honneur (ah **fehr** doh **nuhr**) a matter of honor or principle; a duel.

> A really sure fix on [Bob] Hope's land would mean sending a professional appraiser out personally to step off each parcel. A series of appraisers, in fact, since no one in California could have the necessary feel for the marketplace in so many places at once. It would cost a fortune, but that didn't matter. This was an *affaire d'honneur.*
>
> —RICHARD BEHAR, *Forbes*

affiche (ah **feesh**) a public notice or advertisement affixed to a wall.

> Someone I care about a lot has put an *affiche* on the door to her office at the local university announcing: "Yes, Martin Peretz is an old and beloved friend. No, I am not responsible for his politics."
>
> —MARTIN PERETZ, *The New Republic*

à froid (ah **fwah**) in cold blood.

à gauche (ah **gohsh**) on the left.

agent provocateur (**ah** zhah^n proh voh kah **tuhr**) one who incites another to commit a criminal act; a political agitator.

> I asked for yogurt. They gave me a West German brand, but I could see they had an East German product as well, so I asked for that. Consternation. They looked at me as if I were either a fool or an *agent provocateur.* Why would anyone eat East German yogurt when they could have West German for only twice the price? So I bought one of each and tasted both. They were both awful. Conclusion: eat neither.
>
> —ARPAD LAZAR, *Harvard Business Review*

à gogo (ah **goh** goh) in abundance; galore; in a fast and lively manner. The term was common in fifteenth-century France, fell into disuse, and was reintroduced in 1947 through a book by Sir Compton Mackenzie entitled *Whisky Galore,* the French translation of which is *Whisky à gogo.* It came to America in the 1960s as the name of a rock nightclub on the Sunset Strip in Los Angeles, and in the term *go-go dancer,* a girl in a *discothèque* who stands on a platform or in a cage, wears white plastic boots, and does the "swim," the "frug," the "jerk," and the "monkey."

à grands frais (ah grah^n **fray**) at great expense.

agrément (ah gray **mah^n**) pleasure; enjoyment.

agréments de la vie (ah gray **mah^n** duh lah **vee**) the refinements of life; the amenities; the pleasures.

à huis clos (ah wee **kloh**) behind closed doors; in secret.

aide de camp (**ehd** duh **kah^n**) an officer in attendance on a general; any officer assigned as an assistant to a superior, and by analogy a civilian aide to an executive.

aide-mémoire (**ehd** maym **wahr**) "help to the memory"; a diplomatic memorandum confirming previous discussions; a mnemonic device.

> When [John] Ruskin advised young artists to use daguerreotypes in their work, he was not proposing photography as a substitute for the skill of draughtsmanship and the science of perspective; he was assuming that academically trained artists would use the camera as an *aide-memoire*, an adjunct to drawing, not a replacement for it.
>
> —RICHARD DORMENT, *Daily Telegraph*

aigrette (ay **gret**) "egret"; a plume of feathers; a spray of gems resembling a plume.

à la (**ah** lah) in the manner or style of; as prepared for or by. This term is useful shorthand for expressing similarity or imitation. Thus *à la Tartuffe*, "in the style or manner of Tartuffe," denotes someone like Tartuffe, the piously hypocritical title character of a Molière comedy. But *à la* is probably more familiar to English speakers as a culinary term, as in "chicken *à la king*." See also, *à la mode*.

à l'ancienne (ah lah^n **syen**) in the old style; old-fashioned.

à l'abandon (ah lah bah^n **do^n**) with abandon; carelessly; without inhibition.

à la belle étoile (ah lah **bel** ay **twahl**) "under the beautiful star"; under the night sky.

à la bonne heure (ah lah bun **uhr**) at the right time; well done!; way to go!

à la carte (ah lah **kart**) "on the card"; according to the menu; each item ordered and paid for individually. Cf. *table d'hôte, prix fixe.*

à la française (ah lah frah^n **sez**) in the French style.

> The Folies Bergère, founded in 1869, gave American G.I.s their first glimpse of glamour *à la française.* It has showcased some beautiful legs—[Josephine] Baker's were insured at the time for $100,000.
>
> —MARILYN AUGUST, *Toronto Star*

à la grecque (ah lah **grek**) in the Greek style.

à la guerre comme à la guerre (ah lah **gehr** kum ah lah **gehr**) "In war as in war"; one must take the good with the bad.

à la lanterne! (ah lah lah^n **tehrn**) "To the lamppost!" The streets of eighteenth-century Paris were lit by lamps hung from the walls of buildings. The *lanterne de la Grève*, above a grocery in the *Place de la Grève*, was used for summary executions immediately after the fall of the *Bastille* (which see) in July of 1789. Hence "To the lamppost!", a revolutionary cry meaning "let them hang from the lamppost," often in the form of *"Les aristocrates a la lanterne!"* See also, *au poteau!*

> I learn from Ian Hamilton's review . . . that Tom Paulin, Reader in Poetry at the University of Nottingham, has just published a book in which he asserts that "Official Standard English" belongs "with the State's hardware, its myths and slogans and lies." Furthermore, he alleges that "Standard punctuation enforces the power of certain institutionalised values." Will it soon be *à la lanterne* for all those who use the apostrophe correctly?
>
> —JUNE BASSETT, *Sunday Telegraph* (London)

à la lyonnaise (ah lah lyo^n **nez**) in the style of Lyon, i.e., cooked with sliced onions.

à l'américaine (ah lah may ree **ken**) in the American style.

à la militaire (ah lah mee lee **tehr**) in military style.

à la mode (ah lah **mohd**) according to the prevailing mode; in the current style; in fashion. In the United States it also means "with ice cream," as in "apple pie *à la mode.*"

> To those of us who were alive and sartorially active at the time, it was saddening to read in the *Boston Globe* recently the allegation, by "New York Socialite" Susan Rosenstiel, that in 1958 J. Edgar Hoover was parading around in a Plaza Hotel suite wearing women's clothes: "He was wearing a fluffy black dress, very fluffy, with flounces, and lace stockings and high heels, and a black curly wig." I was saddened to think that future generations, trying to grasp the peculiar splendor and excitement of high-echelon cross-dressing during Eisenhower's second term, will imagine that dowdy bit of black fluff, with its fussy flounces and matching wig, to have been *très à la mode*, when the truth is we all considered J. Edgar Hoover something of a frump.
>
> —JOHN UPDIKE, *The New Yorker*

à l'anglaise (ah lah^n **glez**) in the English style.

> The French are fond of saying that they are more tolerant of, say, infidelity and adultery than are the Anglo-Saxons, and that the law simply reflects this relaxed attitude. In fact, they gossip, are extremely censorious and, although there is no tabloid press *à l'anglaise*, there is a thriving glitter-gutter press in the shape of "human interest" magazines, glossiest of which is *Paris Match*.
>
> —*Daily Telegraph* (London)

à la page (ah lah **pahzh**) up-to-date; in the know; in fashion.

à la parisienne (ah lah pah ree **zyen**) in the Parisian style.

à la provençale (ah lah proh vah^n **sahl**) cooked with garlic or onions.

À la recherche du temps perdu (ah lah ruh **shehrsh** dü tah^n pehr **dü**) "In search of lost time," the title of the monumental novel by Marcel Proust (1871–1922) published in seven volumes between 1913 and 1927 and loosely translated as *Remembrance of Things Past*. The autobiographical narrator,

Marcel, transcends time through involuntary memories evoked by sensations or moods. The dense, complex novel often employs *monologue intérieur* (which see) to examine the connection between memory and reality. Because of its length and difficulty, *À la recherche du temps perdu* is perhaps the least read Great Book in Western culture.

à la rigueur (ah lah ree **guhr**) if absolutely necessary; strictly speaking.

à la russe (ah lah **rüs**) in the Russian style.

à la viennoise (ah lah vyen **wahz**) in the Viennese style.

à l'espagnole (ah les pah **nyohl**) in the Spanish style.

à l'impériale (ah lam pay **ryahl**) in the (British) imperial style.

à l'improviste (ah lam proh **veest**) suddenly; unexpectedly.

à l'italienne (ah lee tahl **yen**) in the Italian style.

alouette (**ah** loo et) lark; the title of a popular French children's song.

à l'outrance (ah loo **trahn**s) to the utmost; to the bitter end; to the death. In this case the Frenglish is grammatically incorrect: *à outrance* is proper French.

amant (ah **mahn**) lover.

amant de coeur (ah **mahn** duh **kuhr**) "heart's lover"; favorite lover.

âme damnée (**ahm** dah **nay**) "damned soul"; a dupe or tool of another.

âme de boue (**ahm** duh **boo**) "soul of mud"; base; mean-spirited.

âme d'élite (**ahm** day **leet**) a soul destined for special treatment.

âme perdue (**ahm** pehr **dü**) "lost soul."

amende honorable (ah **mah**ⁿd ohn oh **rah** bluh) public apology; amends; reparations.

à merveille (ah mehr **vay**) marvelously; wonderfully.

ami de cour (ah **mee** duh **koor**) "court friend"; false or superficial friend.

amie (ah **mee**) mistress; girlfriend.

amitié amoureuse (ah mee **tyay** ah moo **ruhz**) a loving friendship.

> Thomas Hardy signed himself "your rather gloomy and affectionate friend" in a letter to Florence Henniker, the novelist, with whom he carried on an *amitié amoureuse* for some 30 years, and to whom he could write more freely than to either of his wives.
>
> —SYLVIA CLAYTON, *Manchester Guardian Weekly*

amour (ah **moor**) love; love affair.

> Oh, what a dear ravishing thing is the beginning of an *Amour*!
>
> —APHRA BEHN, *The Emperor of the Moon*, Act I, Scene 1

amour courtois (ah **moor** koor **twah**) courtly love; a medieval invention of the courts of France arising from the lyric poetry of the troubadours, it is generally acknowledged as the precursor of the Western notion of romantic love. Basically, *amour courtois* involves the worship of a beautiful and virtuous woman from afar and the suitor's attempt to win her favor through acts of chivalry and prowess.

amour de voyage (ah **moor** duh vwah **yahzh**) a brief infatuation, such as one aboard ship.

amourette (**ah** moor et) "little love"; an insignificant love affair, sometimes with the connotation of "puppy love."

amour-propre (ah **moor proh** pruh) self-love; self-esteem.

> The later [Kurt] Vonnegut novels are deserts, punctuated by the odd paradisal oasis. These good moments are, simply, reversions to his earlier manner, which is why it is more fun to re-read an old Vonnegut novel than it is to tackle a new one. I switched on

the tape-recorder and backed myself into the Big Question. Of all the writers I have met, Vonnegut gives off the mildest prickle of *amour-propre*. But no writer likes to be asked if he has lost his way.

—MARTIN AMIS, "Kurt Vonnegut: After the Slaughterhouse"

ancien régime (ah^n sye^n ray **zheem**) "old regime"; the Bourbon monarchy, overthrown during the French Revolution in 1789, and by analogy any discredited, displaced order.

During the eighteenth century Europeans and colonists in the Americas began speaking of themselves as personally aligned with the entire run of the century into which they were born. They believed they were creatures of their century, with whose spirit they were willy-nilly invested. The century had at last a zeitgeist, which reflected and informed the lives of its natives. When the French Revolution after 1789 deepened the centurial divide between the *ancien régime* and the "modern" world of the next, the nineteenth century, Romantics began to write of a *mal du siècle*, a motion sickness caused by the tumultuous change in centuries. The stark brutalities and reversals of the French Revolution encouraged a habit of historical comparison between the end of one century and the start of the next.

—HILLEL SCHWARTZ, *The New Republic*

animateur (ahn ee mah **tuhr**) a writer who presents difficult material in an understandable form; a popularizer. Synonymous with *vulgarisateur*.

aperçu (ah pehr **sü**) "rapid view"; general survey; intuitive understanding; insight.

Our host [Clive James] punctuates the footage with a string of dry, stinging *aperçus* and observations. To wit, of Nelson Eddy and Jeanette MacDonald: "Each had the uncanny gift of removing all signs of life from the other." Of Adolf Hitler's blustering speeches at Nazi rallies: "To the detached observer he looked like a 6-year-old boy throwing a tantrum in tight underpants."

—DAVID HILTBRAND, *People*

apéritif (ah **pay** ree **teef**) appetizer; a before-dinner drink.

à pied (ah **pyay**) on foot.

à point (ah **pwa**^{n}) in the nick of time; in cooking, done to the point of perfection (i.e., removed from the fire "in the nick of time").

Appellation Contrôlée (ah pel ah **syo**^{n} **ko**^{n} troh **lay**) the official designation for the highest quality French wines.

appliqué (ah plee **kay**) a form of needlework in which pieces of one material are affixed to another.

après coup (**ah** pray **koo**) after the event; too late.

après moi le déluge (**ah** pray **mwah** luh **day** lyüzh) "After me, the deluge." The statement, most often attributed to King Louis XV (1710–74), was also made by the Austrian statesman Prince Metternich (1773–1859) to suggest that the existing political and social order would disintegrate after his death.

après nous le déluge (**ah** pray **noo** luh **day** lyüzh) "After us, the deluge." Attributed to Madame de Pompadour (1721–64), mistress of Louis XV, who is said to have made the remark either after the French defeat by Frederick the Great at Rossbach, or in response to criticism of royal extravagance. In any case the expression is an old French saying.

à propos (apropos) (ah proh **poh**) opportunely; relevant to; regarding.

> Captain Faucon came quietly up to me, as I was at work, with my knife, cutting the meat from a dirty hide, asked me how I liked California, and repeated—*Tityre, tu patulae recubans sub tegmine fagi.* Very *apropos*, thought I, and, at the same time, serves to show that you understand Latin.
>
> —RICHARD HENRY DANA, JR., *Two Years Before the Mast*

French . . . is, perhaps, the most perspicuous and pointed language in the world.
—SAMUEL TAYLOR COLERIDGE, *Miscellaneous*, 1811

à propos de bottes (ah proh **poh** duh **boht**) "speaking of boots"; by the way; to change the subject completely. Synonymous with *à propos de rien*.

à propos de rien (ah proh **poh** duh ree e^n) "relevant to nothing"; by the way; to change the subject completely. Synonymous with *à propos de bottes*.

arabesque (ah rah **besk**) in ballet, a position in which the body is bent forward while standing on one leg with one arm extended forward and the other arm and leg extended backward; in art, an ornate floral pattern or design; in music, a short composition containing numerous embellished passages; in general, any complex pattern or design.

à rebours (ah ruh **boor**) against the grain; against nature; perversely. *A rebours* is the title of J. K. Huysmans' 1884 novel in which the hero, Des Esseintes, seeks to overcome his *ennui* through sensual and aesthetic experiences such as having the shell of a tortoise encrusted with jewels and watching the animal crawl across a carpet.

armoire (arm **wahr**) a freestanding wardrobe or cabinet. From the Old French *armaire*, "chest."

arrière (ah **ryehr**) "rear"; behind the times; old-fashioned.

arrière-garde (ah **ryehr gahrd**) rear guard.

> The string bikini that bares all, the thin film of Lycra that stretches over the body concealing nothing—these glorifications of the natural woman on the beach are now part of the *arrière-garde*. The bra is back in swimsuits.
>
> —BERNADINE MORRIS, *New York Times*

arrière-goût (ah **ryehr goo**) a (usually unpleasant) aftertaste.

arrière-pensée (ah **ryehr** pah^n **say**) ulterior motive.

arrivé (ah ree **vay**) the state of having arrived; successful.

arriviste (ah ree **veest**) "arriver"; social climber; upstart. Cf. *Bourgeois Gentilhomme*, *nouveau riche*, and *parvenu*.

"The Beats Are Back," according to a recent cover story in *New York* magazine. As young poets with first-growth goatees and *poseurs* in new berets fill the bars and coffee houses of the '90s with *arriviste* angst, the North Beach Repertory Theatre has gone back to the source.

—STEVEN WINN, *San Francisco Chronicle*

arrondissement (ah ro^n dees mah^n) a municipal subdivision in some large French cities, including Paris; roughly synonymous with "quarter."

art brut (ahr brüt) art in the raw; outsider art; the untutored, unself-conscious art of amateurs. The term was coined in 1945 by the French painter and sculptor Jean Dubuffet (1901–85) to describe the crude pictures made by children, the elderly, and even mental patients, suggesting that such work, and not the output of trained professionals, is the essence of "true" art.

Basquiat's work as a whole is less *art brut* than art cute. Where Jean Dubuffet (one of his influences) crushes figures into crusty road kills, Basquiat turns his into almost decorative little glyphs and sticks them into nicely boxed compositions that are no scarier than an episode of "The Simpsons."

—PETER PLAGENS and FARAI CHIDEYA, *Newsweek*

art deco (ahr deh koh) a decorative Parisian style popular in the 1920s and 1930s characterized by bold colors and curved lines (also known as *art moderne*).

art engagé (ahr a^n gah zhay) art produced with a political or social motive.

art moderne (ahr moh dehrn) see *art deco*.

art nouveau (ahr noo voh) "new art"; a modernist decorative style that flourished in late-nineteenth- and early-twentieth-century Europe. Characterized by flowing lines and floral motifs, *art nouveau* had a resurgence of popularity in the 1960s and 1970s.

l'art pour l'art (lahr poor lahr) "Art for art's sake," a nineteenth-century notion that art should be created for no ulterior purpose, it was a rallying cry for Gautier, Flaubert, and Baudelaire, among others. The Latin version, *ars gratia artis*, is the mendacious motto of Metro-Goldwyn-Mayer.

art rupestre (**ahr** rü pes truh) prehistoric cave murals.

art sacré (ahr **sah** kray) "sacred art"; a twentieth-century attempt to reestablish religious art.

art trouvé (**ahr** troo **vay**) "found art"; art consisting of objects found in and shaped by nature, such as items washed up on a seashore.

assemblage (**ah** sahm **blahzh**) a technique whereby miscellaneous elements (including metal, cloth, bits of string, and various other *objets trouvés*) are arranged into a three-dimensional work of art. The first *assemblage* so called is Picasso's *Glass of Absinthe* (1914).

atelier (ah tel **yay**) workshop; a studio where an established artist trains students or apprentices. From the Old French *astelier*, "carpenter's shop."

atelier libre (ah tel **yay lee** bruh) a studio where nude models are provided.

attaché (ah tah **shay**) a member of the staff of a diplomatic mission or embassy assigned to a specific task, e.g., a military *attaché*; a briefcase. From *attacher*, "to attach."

attentat aux moeurs (ah tah^n **tah** oh **muhrs**) an offense against public decency; an indecent attack.

attrapé (ah trah **pay**) "well caught"; a good imitation.

auberge (oh **behrzh**) inn; tavern.

aubergine (oh behr **zheen**) eggplant.

au contraire (oh ko^n **trehr**) on the contrary.

Armed robbery always has amounted to a creative challenge in Texas, and we Texans like to believe we've added our own artful nuances to the concept. Consider the San Antonio robber who, just last year, leaped onto one of those small tourist boats that gently cruise the river. He figured he'd ditched a San Antonio policeman who was in hot pursuit. *Au contraire!* The officer valiantly leaped onto the next passing tourist boat, commandeered the vessel and ultimately ended the river chase by running down the criminal.

—JOHN ANDERS, *Dallas Morning News*

au courant (oh koo **rah**^{n}) "in the swim"; up-to-date; with it.

What you don't want to be is *au courant.*

—PETER TAYLOR'S advice to writers

au désespoir (oh **dayz** es **pwahr**) in despair.

au fait (oh **fay**) to the point; competent; well informed; up-to-date.

Sir,—I fully support Mr Roycroft in his plea . . . for dropping the dreary Doonesbury cartoon strip. For far too long, it has been (a) rarely amusing, (b) from time to time distinctly tasteless, and (c) to those not *au fait* with American social and political life, usually incomprehensible.

—J. STANLEY TREANOR, letter to the *Irish Times*

au fond (oh **fo**^{n}) at bottom; fundamentally.

au grand galop (oh **grah**^{n} gah **loh**) at full gallop.

au gratin (oh grah **ta**^{n}) topped with browned cheese or bread crumbs.

au naturel (oh nah tü **rehl**) "as in nature"; unadorned; uncooked; in the nude.

au grand sérieux (oh **grah**^{n} say **ryuh**) in all seriousness.

au pair (oh **pehr**) "at par"; without wages; an arrangement whereby a young house servant receives room and board but no monetary payment.

The plan had been that Rhoda's mother would give them the money as a sort of baby present to hire a baby nurse for four weeks, while Rhoda got back on her feet and went back to work. In the meantime, they would find an *au pair* girl to live in and look after the baby in return for room and board. Rhoda's mother had come through with her part of the plan, but it was already obvious that this *au pair* girl who was willing to sleep on a convertible couch in the living room in an ant colony on the West Side did not exist.

—TOM WOLFE, *The Bonfire of the Vanities*

au pied de la lettre (oh **pyay** duh lah **leh** truh) literally.

au poteau! (oh poh **toh**) "To the post!"; a revolutionary phrase meaning "let them hang." See also, *à la lanterne!*

au premier coup (oh pruh **myay koo**) "at first blow"; in one decisive stroke; an oil painting technique in which the final effect is achieved with a single application of paint (as opposed to covering the canvas layer by layer).

au premier coup d'oeil (oh pruh **myay koo** doy) at first glance.

au reste (oh **rest**) "for the rest"; besides.

au revoir (oh **vwahr**) good-bye; till we meet again.

au sérieux (oh say **ryuh**) seriously; earnestly.

aussitôt dit, aussitôt fait (oh see toh **dee**, oh see toh **fay**) No sooner said than done.

auteur (oh **tuhr**) "author"; creator. *La politique des auteurs* is the theory that a film's director is its primary creative influence, its true "author," an idea advanced by various young French critic/filmmakers in the 1950s, beginning with François Truffaut in a 1954 *Cahiers du cinéma* article. The theory gained currency in the United States after it was endorsed by the American critic Andrew Sarris in a 1962 *Film Culture* magazine article.

As *auteurs* continue to unexpurgate their works, the audience's threshold for added footage will be tested. In the meantime, the most prudent recourse may be to a bigger popcorn bowl and a very comfortable couch.

—ANN HORNADAY, *New York Times*

avoir le cafard

autocritique (oh toh kree **teek**) self-criticism.

autres temps, autres moeurs (**oh** truh tah^n, **zoh** truh **muhrs**) "Other days, other ways."

au vif (oh **veef**) "from life"; painted from a living model.

aux armes! (oh **zahrm**) To arms!

avant-garde (ah vah^n **gahrd**) "vanguard"; originally the advance elements of a military force, the term is now applied to innovation or experimentation in the arts.

> Charles Ellik slowly revolves, chanting his ever-mutating verse while he creates existential clacks on a hand-held noisemaker. Throughout the tiny theater, other poets begin to clap in unison. They are here to ride the latest wave in the *avant-garde* "performance poetry," itself an ever-mutating, vaguely defined product of the coffeehouse scene.
>
> —DAVID FERRELL, *Los Angeles Times*

avant-goût (ah vah^n **goo**) foretaste.

avec plaisir (ah **vehk** play **zeer**) with pleasure.

avoir le cafard (ah **vwahr** luh kah **fahr**) to be depressed; to have the blues (literally, "to have the cockroach").

à votre santé (ah **voh** truh sah^n **tay**) "To your health" (used as a toast).

b

baba au rhum (bah **bah** oh **ruhm**) a plum cake soaked in rum, a dessert said to have originated with a Polish king exiled in France who drenched a dry cake with rum and named the concoction after his favorite fictional hero, Ali Baba in *Arabian Nights*.

baccalauréat (bah kah loh ray **ah**) in France, a pre-university examination and degree. The French seldom use the word anymore, but abbreviate it to *bachot* (bah **shoh**).

baccarat (bah kah **rah**) a card game similar to *chemin de fer*, the object of which is to hold cards totaling nine (with face cards and tens equaling zero).

bacchanale (bah kah **nahl**) drunken orgy.

badinage (bah dee **nahzh**) banter; playfulness; child's play. From *badin*, "joker."

> *Immortality* teems with the freewheeling philosophical ***badinage*** that captivated readers of *The Unbearable Lightness of Being* (1984). Kundera's aphorisms, observations and definitions continue to provoke: "The face is only the serial number of a specimen"; "Public opinion polls are a parliament in permanent session"; . . . "Every woman prefers her child to her husband."
>
> —CARLIN ROMANO, *Philadelphia Inquirer*

badinerie (bah deen **ree**) a fast, playful musical piece popular in the eighteenth century.

bagatelle (bah gah **tel**) bauble; trifle; trifling amount.

> They may talk of a comet, or a burning mountain, or some such ***bagatelle***; but, to me, a modest woman, drest out in all her finery, is the most tremendous object of the whole creation.
>
> —OLIVER GOLDSMITH, *She Stoops to Conquer*

baguette (bah **get**) stick; baton; rod; an oblong-shaped jewel; a similarly shaped loaf of bread.

baignoire (ben **wahr**) bathtub; a theater box.

bain-marie (ba^n mah ree) "Mary's bath"; a double boiler used to keep sauces warm.

ballade (bah **lahd**) a French verse form popular in the fourteenth and fifteenth centuries.

ballon d'essai (**bah** lo^n deh **say**) trial balloon.

bal masqué (bahl mahs **kay**) masked ball.

banalité (bah nah lee **tay**) triteness; triviality.

banc (bah^{n}k) seat; judge's bench.

bandeau (bah^n **doh**) a thin strip of material; a headband; a blindfold.

banquette (bah^n **ket**) a cushioned bench, usually in a restaurant; a window seat.

baroque (bah **rohk**) a rich, dynamic style of European art and architecture dominant during the seventeenth century, characterized by bold forms and elaborate ornamentation.

barre (bahr) in ballet, a waist-high practice bar mounted along a wall, usually in front of a mirror.

batiste (bah **teest**) a delicate, plain-woven fabric used in a variety of garments.

bâton (bah **to**^{n}) stick; cudgel; the wand used to conduct an orchestra; a jewel *baguette*.

batterie de cuisine (bah **tree** duh kwee **zeen**) a complete set of cooking utensils.

béarnaise (bayr **nez**) a creamy sauce named for Béarn, a town in southwestern France.

beau geste (boh **zhest**) "beautiful gesture"; a grand or magnanimous display; an act of self-sacrificial bravery. Also, the title of a 1924 novel by P. C. Wren and a 1939 movie starring

Gary Cooper, Ray Milland, and Robert Preston as three dashing English brothers who join the French Foreign Legion.

> *BEAU GESTE* IN BOSNIA GOES AWRY; WHEN FRENCH GEN. PHILIPPE MORILLON JOINED THE BESIEGED MUSLIMS OF SREBRENICA, HE BECAME AN INSTANT HERO. BUT HE MISJUDGED THE WORLD'S WILLINGNESS TO FOLLOW HIM.
>
> —HEADLINE, *Los Angeles Times*

beau idéal (**boh** ee day **ahl**) "ideal beauty"; the abstract essence of beauty; a model or paradigm.

> [Clark Gable] was the virile King of Hollywood, the star who embodied the dash of Rhett Butler and the glamour of the movies, at once a man's man and a lady-killer whose personal style became the *beau idéal* of his generation.
>
> —TIM PURTELL, *Entertainment Weekly*

beau monde (boh mo^{n}d) "beautiful world"; the world of high society and fashion.

> [Frederick] Hughes raised Warhol from the *demi-monde* to the *beau monde*, turning The Factory, Warhol's bohemian backdrop, into a money-spinning organisation and encouraging the rich, titled and famous to have their portraits painted by Warhol.
>
> —KATE BERNARD, *Sunday Times* (London)

beaux arts (boh **zahr**) the fine arts, characterized by formalism and a tendency toward monumental design, particularly in architecture.

bel âge (beh **lahzh**) advanced age.

bel air (beh **lehr**) fine carriage; poise.

(La) Belle Dame sans Merci ([lah] bel dahm **sah**^{n} mehr see) "The Beautiful Lady without Mercy," the title of a ballad by John Keats, published in 1820, derived from a French poem by Alain Chartier.

bel esprit (bel es **pree**) brilliant wit.

> If [Pat] Sajak is the guarded wit, [David] Letterman the sharp-tongued cynic and [Johnny] Carson the smooth, gray-haired *bel*

esprit, then [Arsenio] Hall is the playful gallant, the rascal with enough green to get away with almost anything.

—MICHAEL NORMAN, *New York Times*

belle amie (bel ah **mee**) lady friend; mistress.

belle époque (bel ay **pohk**) "beautiful era"; the period between 1890 and the beginning of World War I, nostalgically remembered as a time of European affluence and gentility.

For many years, the century's codified nostalgia was all but monopolised by the *belle époque*, a halcyon period when parasols seemed to be more common than umbrellas and butterflies than flies.

—GILBERT ADAIR, *Sunday Times* (London)

belle laide (bel **lehd**) a physically unattractive woman who somehow transcends her appearance to achieve a strange allure. Synonymous with *jolie laide*.

belle mort (**bel** mohr) natural death.

belle peinture (**bel** pa^n tür) traditional, representational painting (as opposed to modern art).

belles lettres (bel **let** ruh) "beautiful writing"; serious literature, including poetry and criticism.

The prose poem emanating from a wilderness trek or canoe trip has become a staple of contemporary American *belles lettres*. Its practitioners include such artful essayists as Edward Hoagland, Annie Dillard, Edward Abbey and Barry Lopez—and a host of less skillful rhapsodists.

—DENNIS DRABELLE, *Smithsonian*

béret (bay **ray**) a circular, brimless cap often worn at an angle.

bête noire (bet **nwahr**) "black beast"; something or someone that evokes fear and loathing.

In 1985, an extraordinary reversal took place: 40 years after abject defeat and occupation at the hands of the U.S. army, Japan became the largest creditor nation on earth; simultaneously, America became the biggest debtor. Golf courses, condominiums, the Exxon and Rockefeller buildings fell to Japanese real estate companies and, as the 50th anniversary of Pearl Harbor approached, America discovered its new *bête noir.*

—RICHARD LLOYD PARRY, *Daily Telegraph* (London)

bêtise (bay **teez**) nonsense; foolishness; stupidity.

bibelot (**beeb** loh) curio; knickknack; bauble; a miniature book.

bidet (bee **day**) a toiletlike porcelain fixture for bathing the private parts.

bien élevé (bye^n nay leh **vay**) well brought up.

> Anthony Burstall has lived in France for 38 years. Tall, distinguished and grey-haired, he is always described as *sympathique* and *bien élevé*, a real gent. Such distinctions are very much alive in republican France. Indeed, they can be a veritable minefield: *nuance* is a very French word.
>
> —R. W. F. POOLE, *Daily Telegraph* (London)

bien entendu (bye^n nah^n tah^n **dü**) well understood; certainly; of course.

bien être (bye^n neh **truh**) well-being.

bien pensant (bye^n pah^n **sah^n**) right-minded; orthodox.

> [Vikram] Seth may not be a magic realist, but he is inescapably one of midnight's children. Perhaps partly for this reason, he's also often resented in his country of birth, where *bien pensant* rationalism can be written off as inauthentic, Westernized, and insipid.
>
> —CHRISTOPHER HITCHENS, *Vanity Fair*

bien trouvé (bye^n troo **vay**) well conceived.

bien vu (bye^n **vü**) well regarded; esteemed.

bijou (bee **zhoo**) jewel; jewelry; gem; trinket.

billet (bee **yay**) ticket; note.

billet doux (bee yay **doo**) love letter.

bistro (bees **troh**) a small tavern or restaurant where wine is served. While its exact origin is unknown, *bistro* was first recorded in French in the late nineteenth century, and entered English in the 1920s. According to one story, it comes from a Russian word: After the fall of Napoleon in 1815, Russian troops frequenting Parisian cafés shouted, *"Bystro, bystro,"* "Quickly, quickly." Or, it may stem from the French word *bistouille*, a blend of coffee and alcohol.

bizarrerie (bee zah reh **ree**) grotesquerie; weirdness.

> Very polished languages, and such as are praised for their superior clearness and perspicuity, are generally deficient in strength. The French language has that perfection and that defect.
> —EDMUND BURKE, *The Sublime and Beautiful*, 1756

blagueur (blah **guhr**) braggart; practical joker.

blancmange (blahnk **mahnzh**) a jellied almond pudding.

bloc (blohk) "block"; a political alliance or coalition.

boîte (bwaht) box; case; a dive; a joint; an intimate little club.

boîte de nuit (bwaht duh **nwee**) nightclub.

bombé (bohm **bay**) rounded; curved (usually in reference to furniture).

bon appétit (bo^n nah pay **tee**) "good appetite"; enjoy your meal!

bon avocat, mauvais voisin (bo^n nah voh **kah**, moh vay **vwah** sa^n) "Good lawyer, bad neighbor."

bonbon (bo^n bo^n) a sweet; candy.

bonbonnière (bo^n bo^n **nyehr**) a candy box or dish; a candy shop. Figuratively, a cozy little house or apartment.

bon bourgeois (bo^n boor **zhwah**) upstanding citizen.

bon chic, bon genre (bo^n **sheek,** bo^n **zhah^n** ruh) literally, "good style, good manners"; figuratively, "preppy."

> In Paris the BCBGs—**bon chic, bon genre**, the French equivalent of American preppies—lace their sneakers with the signature brown-and-white cotton ribbons used to tie Hermes gift boxes.
>
> —HOLLY BRUBACH, *The Atlantic*

bon copain (bo^n koh **pa^n**) good companion; loyal friend.

bon enfant (bo^n nah^n **fah^n**) good child; a good-natured fellow.

bon goût (bo^n **goo**) good taste.

bon gré, mal gré (bo^n gray, **mahl** gray) "[with] good grace or ill-grace"; willy-nilly.

bonhomie (boh noh **mee**) good nature; warm-heartedness.

> John Stuart Mill
> By a mighty effort of will
> Overcame his natural *bonhomie*
> And wrote *Principles of Political Economy*.
>
> —EDMUND CLERIHEW BENTLEY

bonhomme (boh **nohm**) a chap; a fellow; a simple, good-natured man.

bon marché (bo^n mar **shay**) good bargain; inexpensive; the name of a well-known department store in Paris.

bon mot (bo^n **moh**) a clever remark; a witticism; an epigram.

> It seems [James McNeill] Whistler had grown tired of hearing his witticisms repeated around London by [Oscar] Wilde, who often received credit for them. One day Wilde was so impressed with a *bon mot* uttered by Whistler he said, "Oh, Jimmy, I wish I had said that."
>
> "You will, Oscar," Whistler replied. "You will."
>
> —DAVID FRIEDMAN, *Newsday*

bonne amie (bun ah **mee**) girlfriend; sweetheart.

bonne foi (bun **fwah**) good faith.

bonnes fortunes (bun fohr **tün**) romantic or sexual triumphs.

bonnet rouge (buh nay **roozh**) the red bonnet worn by French revolutionaries, and hence any revolutionary.

bon sens (bo^n **sah^{n}s**) good sense; common sense.

bon ton (bo^n **to^n**) good breeding.

bon vivant (bo^n vee **vah^n**) one who enjoys good living, especially fine food and wine.

> [Dean Martin] Rat-Packed and six-packed, patenting the image of the blotto *bon vivant*.
>
> —RICHARD CORLISS, *Time*

bon viveur (bo^n vee **vuhr**) loose liver; man about town.

bon voyage (bo^n vwah **yahzh**) (have a) good trip.

bordelaise (bohr duh **lez**) "from Bordeaux"; a sauce made with red wine and shallots.

bouche bée (**boosh** bay) "mouth wide open" to express shock or astonishment.

boudoir (boo **dwahr**) a woman's dressing room, sitting room, or small bedroom.

bouffant (boo **fah^n**) "puffed up"; a hairstyle popular in the 1960s.

bouillabaisse (boo yuh **bess**) an elaborate Provençal fish stew.

bouillion (boo **yo^n**) clear broth or stock.

boulevardier (bool var **dyay**) one who frequents the cafés and bistros along the boulevards; a pleasure-seeker; a lounger.

bouleversement (**boo** luh vehrs **mah^n**) a violent upset; a tumult; a complete reversal. From *bouleverser*, "to overturn."

bourgeois (boor **zhwah**) a member of the urban middle class; someone with conventional values; uncultured; materialistic.

> Consumer culture is making inroads into communist China. The Great Hall of the People is on its way to becoming the great

boulevardier

"mall" of the people, as China's new rich enjoy the spoils of *bourgeois* culture.

—MIKE CHINOY, CNN International News

Bourgeois Gentilhomme (boor **zhwah** zhahn tee **yohm**) "middle-class gentleman"; a would-be gentleman; a *parvenu*; from *Le Bourgeois Gentilhomme*, a play by Molière (1670), in which the title character, an ignorant *bourgeois*, tries to become a gentleman but succeeds only in making himself a laughingstock.

bourgeoisie (boor zhwah **zee**) the middle class; in Marxist theory, the capitalist class opposing the proletariat in the class struggle.

boutonné (boo toh **nay**) "buttoned up"; reticent; laconic.

The popular image of the Oxbridge don is of a bent, crabbed, *boutonné* figure, tightly wrapped in the bonds of his learning, able to communicate easily only with his own kind at high table.

—*The Economist*

boutonnière (boo tun **yehr**) "button-maker"; a flower worn in the buttonhole.

brasserie (brah **sree**) "brewery"; a restaurant where beer is served.

bric-à-brac (**brik** ah brahk) miscellaneous curios; odds and ends.

> It was too sunny a morning to spend in the gloom of a warehouse, and we stayed among the outside stalls under the plane trees where the purveyors of what they like to call *haut bric-à-brac* spread their offerings on tables and chairs or on the ground, or hung them from nails in the tree trunks.
>
> —PETER MAYLE, *A Year in Provence*

brioche (bree **ohsh**) a soft breakfast roll made with egg. The remark attributed to Marie Antoinette on being informed that the populace had no bread, "Let them eat cake," was actually, *"Qu'ils mangent de la brioche."*

briquet (bree **kay**) a block of compressed coal dust or charcoal used for fuel; a cigarette lighter.

brouhaha (**broo** hah hah) uproar; hubbub; sensation; furor.

brut (brüt) crude; unadulterated; an unsweetened wine.

burnoose/burnous (boor **noos**) a hooded cloak.

bustier (büs **tyay**) a sleeveless woman's top worn as lingerie or evening wear.

Gallicisms in the English Language

~

Many French words have penetrated English so thoroughly, and have become so indispensable to English speakers, they hardly seem foreign: amateur, ambiance, aplomb, argot, avalanche, banal, barrage, bastion, bayonet, bivouac, bizarre, blasé, boulevard, bouquet, brochure, brunette, brusque, buffet, bureau, burlesque, butte, café, cajole, camouflage, caprice, carafe, carrousel, cassette, chalet, chandelier, chaperon, charade, chassis, chauffeur, chef, chevron, chic, cinema, cliché, clientele, clique, cologne, concierge, coterie, crèche, critique, croquet, debonnaire, debris, debut, debutante, décor, deluxe, depot, detour, discotheque, divorcée, doctrinaire, dossier, douche, echelon, elite, emigré, enclave, encore, entourage, entrepreneur, expertise, exposé, facade, facile, fiancé, figurine, filet mignon, finesse, foible, fondue, format, fort, forte, fracas, fuselage, gaffe, galant, gigolo, grille, grippe, impasse, insouciance, liqueur, locale, loge, macabre, mannequin, marionnette, massage, matinée, mayonnaise, memoir, meringue, migraine, minuscule, mirage, morale, morgue, motif, mousse, musicale, mystique, naiveté, negligé, parfait, parquet, pâté, pavillon, penchant, percale, perfume, personnel, petite, physique, picaresque, pique, pirouette, plaque, plateau, praline, prestige, promenade, protégé, puree, questionnaire, rappel, rapport, regime, renaissance, repertoire, reportage, reprise, restaurant, résumé, reverie, ricochet, riposte, rococo, role, rotisserie, rouge, roulette, sachet, salon, savant, séance, silhouette, soufflé, souvenir, suave, suede, suite, surveillance, timbre, toupee, tourniquet, trait, tutu, valet, venue, verve, vignette, vogue, *et cetera.*

C

cabaret (**kah** bah ray) a café or nightclub providing live entertainment.

> *Cabaret*, descended over the past century from the *boîtes* of London, Berlin, Paris, and New York itself, makes intimacy into an art.
>
> —WHITNEY BALLIETT, *The New Yorker*

cabinet particulier (kah bee **nay** pahr tee kü **lyay**) a private room in a *de luxe* restaurant; a private room maintained exclusively for trysts.

cache (kahsh) hiding place.

cache-sexe (**kahsh** seks) "hide sex"; a breechcloth or G-string.

cachet (kah **shay**) seal of authority; mark of distinction; prestige.

cadre (**kah** druh) "framework"; nucleus; a core group of trained personnel around which a larger organization may be developed.

cafard (kah **fahr**) "cockroach"; severe depression. See also, *avoir le cafard*.

> Reading old journals, I find that the booze fight and the *cafard* have been going on for longer than I knew.
>
> —JOHN CHEEVER, *The Journals of John Cheever*

café au lait (kah **fay** oh **lay**) coffee made with milk.

café filtre (kah **fay feel** truh) coffee made by pouring boiling water through filtered coffee grounds.

café littéraire (kah **fay** lee tay **rehr**) a coffeehouse frequented by writers.

café noir (kah fay **nwahr**) black coffee.

cahier (kah **yay**) notebook; journal.

Cahiers du Cinéma (kah **yay** dü see nay **mah**) an influential French film journal founded in 1951 that propounded the *auteur* (which see) theory of young critic/filmmakers such as Jean-Luc Godard, Claude Chabrol, and François Truffaut.

ça ira (sah ee **rah**) It will succeed; all will go well; it will be all right. From a 1789 revolutionary song with the refrain:

> *Ah, ça ira, ça ira, ça ira!*
> *Les aristocrates à la lanterne!*

caisson (**kay** so^n) a large box; a horse-drawn vehicle used to carry artillery ammunition, or a casket at a military funeral; a watertight container used in underwater construction.

camaraderie (kahm rah **dree**) comradeship; good fellowship.

canaille (kah **nai**) "pack of dogs"; hoi polloi; rabble; riff-raff.

canapé (kah nah **pay**) a garnished slice of bread or toast served as an appetizer.

canard (kah **nahr**) "duck"; a deliberately misleading story; a hoax; a widely believed fallacy. The idiom may be derived from *vendre un canard à moitié*, to "half-sell a duck," hence, to swindle.

> Once you make a fruitcake you have to give it away, a generous gesture that inevitably gives rise to the old *canard* that there is only one fruitcake in the world and it is passed along each year. Fruitcake bakers have to put up with all sorts of such tired jokes: "Do I eat it or build with it?" Or, "I've worked in an emergency room, I know what fruitcake can do to people."
>
> —LAURA SESSIONS STEPP, *Washington Post*

ça ne fait rien (sahn **fay** ree e^n) it's nothing; it doesn't matter; it isn't important.

capable de tout (kah **pah** bluh duh **too**) capable of anything; unpredictable.

carte blanche (kahrt **blah^{n}sh**) "white card"; complete discretion; a blank paper with only one signature on it, conferring on the recipient the power to dictate whatever terms he wishes. The origin is perhaps military: A victorious commander forces his vanquished opponent to sign a blank piece of paper and then fills in the terms of surrender unilaterally.

> Of all the benefits of spinsterhood, the greatest is *carte blanche*. Once a woman is called "that crazy old maid" she can get away with anything.
>
> —FLORENCE KING, *National Review*

carte de visite (**kahrt** duh vee **zeet**) calling card.

cartel (kahr **tel**) an association of businesses or nations formed to control the production, pricing, and marketing of goods.

cartonnier (**kahr** toh **nyay**) a large, flat cabinet for storing posters, prints, or drawings.

cartouche (kahr **toosh**) a decorative structure or figure used to frame inscriptions. They were often used during the sixteenth and seventeenth centuries on the title pages of books.

cas de conscience (**kah** duh ko^n **syo^{n}s**) "case of conscience"; a moral issue.

ça se sent, ça ne s'explique pas (sah suh **sah^n** sahn **seks** pleek pah) "One can feel it but not explain it"; an all-purpose phrase roughly equivalent to "I can't put it into words." Cf. *je ne sais quoi*.

catalogue raisonné (kah tah **lohg** ray zo^n **nay**) descriptive catalogue; a systematic, descriptive list.

cause célèbre (**kohz** say **leh** bruh) "celebrated case"; something or someone of great public interest; a controversial issue.

> Jack Kevorkian, also known as "Dr. Death," was a retired pathologist when he became a national *cause célèbre* for inventing a suicide machine.
>
> —*U.S. News & World Report*

Ce que tu manges, ce que tu es

causerie (koh **zree**) a chat; an informal interview; a light, breezy essay.

ça va (sah **vah**) all right; okay; good.

ça va sans dire (sah **vah** sah[n] **deer**) "That goes without saying"; obviously.

ce que tu manges, ce que tu es (skuh tü **mahnzh** skuh tü **ay**) "You are what you eat." The famous dictum of France's first great *gastronome*, Jean-Anthelme Brillat-Savarin (1755–1826), from his witty disquisition on the art of dining, *Physiologie du goût* (1825). The phrase is sometimes quoted in its longer, original version: *"Dis-moi ce que tu manges, et je dirai ce que tu es,"* "Tell me what you eat, and I will tell you what you are."

cercle privé (**sehr** kluh pree **vay**) private circle; intimate group.

c'est à dire (**say** tah **deer**) that is to say; namely.

c'est l'amour (**say** lah **moor**) That's love.

c'est la vie (say lah **vee**) That's life; what can one do?

c'est la guerre (say lah **gehr**) That's war; that's the way it goes.

c'est magnifique (say mahn yee **feek**) That's magnificent.

c'est magnifique, mais ce n'est pas la guerre (say mahn yee **feek,** may suh **neh** pah lah **gehr**) "It's magnificent, but it isn't war"; French general Pierre Bosquet (1810–61) on the suicidal Charge of the Light Brigade at Balaclava (October 25, 1854), and hence any futile display of military heroism.

ce n'est pas une révolte, c'est une révolution (**suh** nay pah zün ray **vohlt,** say tün ray voh lü **syo^n**) "It isn't a riot, it's a revolution." After the storming of the Bastille on July 14, 1789, Louis XVI returned to Versailles from a hunting trip and was greeted by the Duc de La Rochefoucauld-Liancourt, who informed him of the attack. "This is a riot!" said the king. "No sire," replied the nobleman, "it isn't a riot, it's a revolution."

c'est tout dire (say too **deer**) "That's all there is to say"; the last word on the subject.

chacun à son goût (shah **kuhn** ah so^n **goo**) "Everyone has his taste"; tastes differ; to each his own.

chagrin d'amour (shah **gra^n** dah **moor**) the heartbreak of an unhappy love affair.

chaise longue (shez **lo^{n}g**) "long chair"; a sofa with a back- or head-rest.

chantage (shah^n **tahzh**) blackmail.

chanteuse (shah^n **tuhz**) female nightclub singer.

> Like her forebears, who were called *chanteuses*, torch singers, café singers, and saloon singers, [Andrea Marcovici] sings in small rooms to small audiences about evanescent things—a blue moon, a skylark, a cottage for two.
>
> —**WHITNEY BALLIETT,** *The New Yorker*

chapeau rouge (shah **poh** roozh) "red hat"; the red headgear worn by a cardinal of the Catholic Church; the cardinal himself.

charcuterie (shahr kü **tree**) a butcher shop specializing in pork; various cuts of pork.

chargé d'affaires (shahr **zhay** dah **fehr**) a diplomatic officer of lower rank than an ambassador.

château (shah **toh**) "castle"; mansion; county seat: The wines of France are often named after the estate or *château* where they are produced, hence *Château* Margaux, *Château* Lafite, *Château* Latour, etc. If the wine is also bottled on the estate, *Mise du Château* is used.

> A couple of nights later I was sitting alone in Pommeroy's, telling myself a few old legal anecdotes, when to my surprise and delight Nick walked in alone. He sat down and I ordered a bottle of the best *Château* Fleet Street.
>
> —JOHN MORTIMER, *Rumpole and the Honourable Member*

châteaubriand (shah **toh** bree **ahn**) sliced grilled beefsteak served with sauce, named for Vicomte François René de Châteaubriand (1768–1848), French writer and statesman.

châteaux en Espagne (shah **toh** zah^n neh **spahn** yuh) "castles in Spain"; castles in the air; daydreams; fantasies.

châtelaine (shaht **lehn**) lady of the manor; the mistress of a large, important household; a keychain worn at the waist.

chauvinist (shoh va^n **neest**) superpatriot; jingoist; after Nicolas Chauvin, an intrepid soldier in Napoléon's Grande Armée (which see) who was wounded a total of seventeen times and who, as an old veteran, dedicated his life to extolling French *gloire*. Today the term is applied to fanatical allegiance to a group or cause.

chef d'école (shef day **kohl**) the chief proponent of a "school" of art.

chef de cuisine (shef duh kwee **zeen**) head cook.

chef-d'oeuvre (shay **duhv** ruh) "main work"; masterpiece.

> "I guess what I am," Arno Jordan says with a shrug and a smile, "is the Michelangelo of pig painters." If so, Hog Heaven is his Sistine Chapel. For 20 years Jordan has labored on his *chef-*

cherchez la femme

d'oeuvre, painting and restoring a vision of porcine paradise in which swine run free, roll in mud and chomp corncobs on more than 4,000 feet of wall space—the longest commercial mural in the U.S.

—*People*

chemin de fer (shuh **ma**ⁿ duh **fehr**) "railway"; a card game similar to *baccarat.*

chemise (shuh **meez**) "shirt"; a long-bodiced dress or woman's undergarment.

chemise de nuit (shuh **meez** duh **nwee**) a woman's nightgown.

chenille (shuh **nee**) "caterpillar"; a soft, cordlike thread woven into cloth for various garments.

cherchez la femme (**shehr** shay lah **fahm**) "Look for the woman"; there's probably a woman to blame.

There are more than 3,000 species of mosquitoes on the planet, and only a small percentage of these feed on human blood. *Cher-*

chez la femme, alas, for the culprits. Pregnant females need blood protein for their eggs to develop.

—REBECCA BRAGG, *Toronto Star*

chère amie (**shehr** ah **mee**) *politesse* (which see) for mistress.

chéri (shay **ree**) darling.

cheval de bataille (shuh **vahl** duh bah **tai**) "battle horse"; favorite subject; hobbyhorse.

chevalier d'industrie (**shuh** vahl yay da^n dü **stree**) "knight of industry"; an adventurer; a wheeler-dealer.

Unless a man knows French, he is held of little account [in England].

—ROBERT OF GLOUCESTER, *Chronicle*, 1298

---

chevaux de frise (shuh **voh** duh **freez**) "Frisian horses"; a line of metal spikes or broken glass placed on top of a wall to discourage entry.

> Was Dun Aengus once circular? Did the cliff collapse and part of the fort drop into the seething water? Or was it, like one fort in County Clare on the Irish mainland, actually built in the shape of a horseshoe? Was the *chevaux de frise*, an army of pointed stones raised and tilted against oncomers, erected around the ramparts to repel not only armies of wild men but also herds of wild pigs?
>
> —KEVIN CROSSLEY-HOLLAND, *Washington Post*

chez (shay) at the home of; among.

chez la famille (**shay** lah fah **mee**) at the family home; among the family.

chez moi (shay **mwah**) at my house.

chez nous (shay **noo**) at our house.

chicane (shee **kahn**) a trick or artifice; subterfuge; quibbling; a barrier (in auto racing); a hand with no trumps (in bridge).

chien méchant (shee a^n may shah^n) "bad dog"; beware of dog.

chiffonnier (**shee** foh **nyay**) a chest of drawers with a mirror back. From *chiffon*, "a sheer fabric," which itself descends from the Old French *chiffe*, "old rag." Thus a *chiffonnier* is literally an "old rag chest."

chignon (shee nyo^n) a coiled knot of hair worn at the back of the head.

chinoiserie (sheen wahz **ree**) Chinese curio; decoration in the Chinese style.

chinoiseries administratives (sheen wahz **ree** ahd mee nee strah **teev**) red tape.

cinéaste (see nay **ahst**) filmmaker; a cinema enthusiast.

> Sometimes, when I'm making a film, I actually find myself thinking, if I make the next shot just like a certain shot in *American Gigolo*, maybe somebody down the road will notice. You really catch yourself doing it. This is perverse. Should I do this just so some overfed, overwrought *cinéaste* in Omaha can say "Aha!"?
>
> —PAUL SCHRADER, *New York Times*

cinéma vérité (see nay **mah** vay ree **tay**) "camera truth"; realistic film. A filmmaking movement of the 1960s that employed a spontaneous, quasi-documentary style to capture Truth. Practitioners of the genre included D. A. Pennebaker and the Maysles brothers in the United States and Marcel Ophuls in France, whose *The Sorrow and the Pity* is perhaps the most prominent example of the genre.

cinq-à-sept (**sank** ah **set**) "five to seven"; the customary afternoon period for quick assignations, hence the slang, *un petit cinq-à-sept*, roughly equivalent to "matinee."

cire perdue (seer pehr **dü**) "lost wax"; the process of casting bronze in a mold to produce a hollow statue.

citoyen (see twah ya^n) citizen; patriot.

claque (klahk) a group of hired applauders.

claqueur (klah **kuhr**) a hired applauder; a member of a *claque* of professionals hired to applaud (or jeer) at performances. The term probably dates to ancient Rome, when crowds were organized to applaud the emperor Nero.

cloisonné (klwah zoh **nay**) an enameling technique in which different ceramic colors are separated by thin lines of flattened metal.

coiffure (kwah **für**) the style of cutting or dressing hair.

collage (koh **lahzh**) a composition technique in which various materials are pasted onto a flat surface. Cf. *assemblage*.

comédie de moeurs (koh may **dee** duh **muhr**) comedy of manners.

(La) Comédie Française ([lah] koh may **dee** frah^n **sez**) the first state theater of France, founded in 1680.

(la) comédie humaine ([lah] koh may **dee** ü **men**) "(the) human comedy"; the scope of human behavior. From the generic title of a multivolume edition of the novels and short stories of Honoré de Balzac (1799–1850), who intended it as a deliberate (and opposite) reference to Dante's *Divine Comedy*.

comédie larmoyante (koh may **dee** lahr mwah **yah^{n}t**) "tearful comedy"; sentimental drama. A form originated by the Parisian dramatist Pierre-Claude de La Chaussée (1692–1754) that portrays the vicissitudes of domestic life.

> English literature of the time was dominated by sentimental tragedies (Lillo), sentimental comedies (Steele), and sentimental novels (Richardson), while in France the *comédie larmoyante* and *drame bourgeois*, in the hands of such as Diderot, Beaumarchais, and Voltaire, were washing the populace with unguents of delicate feeling and democratic sentiment.
>
> —ROBERT BRUSTEIN, *The New Republic*

comédien (koh may **dya^n**) comedian; actor.

> Most comics never bother to equip themselves as actors. But the best comics are also good actors. Chaplin is a wonderful actor. W. C. Fields and Willie Howard and Bobby Clark were real ac-

tors, and so are Bert Lahr and Joey Adams and Shelley Berman. In France, the word *comédien* actually means both "comedian" and "actor."

—ZERO MOSTEL, *The New Yorker*

comédie noire (koh may **dee nwahr**) "black comedy"; comedy with a tragic tone.

The phone would sometimes be manned by Yelena Bonner's mother, Ruth. In her mid-80's, herself a veteran of 17 years in the gulag and exile, she was a chain smoker with a terrifying cough and a wit that made *comédie noire* look pastel.

—RICHARD LOURIE, *New York Times*

comme ci, comme ça (kum **see** kum **sah**) "like this, like that"; so-so.

comme il faut (**kum** eel **foh**) "as it should be"; in a suitable manner; socially correct behavior.

compère (ko^n **pehr**) master of ceremonies; accomplice; companion; godfather.

confrère (ko^n **frehr**) business or professional associate; colleague.

congé (ko^n **zhay**) permission to depart; official release; discharge.

connoisseur (ko^n nuh **suhr**) a person with refined tastes, especially in the arts.

consommé (ko^n soh **may**) a strong beef broth.

contretemps (ko^n truh **tah**^{n}) "out of time"; a mischance; an accident; a hitch.

In 1991, the IRS auctioned off all of [Willie] Nelson's assets to recoup a portion of the $16.7 million he owed in penalties and interest from an ill-advised tax shelter (Nelson's friends organized and bought up much of the booty with low-ball bids, and held it for him so he'll eventually get it back). The *contretemps* also inspired one of his finest albums, a dark-night-of-the-soul set called "The I.R.S. Tapes—Who'll Buy My Memories?"

—JOE BROWN, *Washington Post*

contrôlé (koⁿ troh lay) controlled; registered; hallmarked.

coquette (koh **ket**) a flirtatious woman.

She *coquetted* with the solid husbands of her friends.

—DOROTHY PARKER

coquille (koh **kee**) shell; scallop.

cordon (kohr **do**ⁿ) string; ribbon; the ring of bubbles that forms inside a glass of sparkling wine.

cordon bleu (kohr **do**ⁿ **bluh**) "blue ribbon"; originally the sash of the Order of *Saint Esprit* ("Holy Ghost") established by Henry III in 1578, it has since come to denote an accomplished cook, or well-prepared and presented food. Also, the name of a renowned Parisian cooking school founded in 1895.

cordon rouge (kohr **do**ⁿ **roozh**) the red sash or ribbon bestowed on recipients of the Légion d'Honneur (which see).

cordon sanitaire (kohr **do**ⁿ **sah** nee **tehr**) a zone or barrier designed to prevent the spread of disease, and by analogy a ring of buffer states around a hostile or potentially dangerous nation.

corps (kohr) "body"; the largest division of an army; a specific group, as in *corps de ballet* (which see).

corps de ballet (**kohr** duh bah **lay**) ballet troupe.

corps diplomatique (**kohr** dee ploh mah **teek**) diplomatic corps; the body of foreign diplomats assigned to a national capital.

cortège (kohr **tehzh**) retinue; a train of attendants; a funeral procession.

côte (koht) coast; shore; hill; slope.

couchette (koo **shet**) a sleeping berth (on a train).

couleur du temps (koo **luhr** dü tah^n) "color of the weather"; the direction the wind is blowing; the prevailing political or social climate.

coup (koo) blow; stroke; knock; tap; a sudden, decisive act; an unexpected success.

coup d'éclat (**koo** day **klah**) "brilliant stroke"; dashing deed.

> As for your choice of subjects, I have only to give you this caution: That as a handsome way of praising is certainly the most difficult point in writing or speaking, I would by no means advise any young man to make his first essay in panegyric, besides the danger of it: for a particular encomium is ever attended with more ill-will, than any general invective, for which I need give no reasons; wherefore, my counsel is, that you use the point of your pen, not the feather; let your first attempt be a *coup d'éclat* in the way of libel, lampoon, or satire. Knock down half a score reputations, and you will infallibly raise your own; and so it be with wit, no matter with how little justice; for fiction is your trade.
>
> —JONATHAN SWIFT, "Letter of Advice to a Young Poet"

coup de foudre (**koo** duh **foo** druh) "thunderstroke"; an immediate and overwhelming passion; love at first sight.

> It was a *coup de foudre*—how do you say in English?—love at first sight. Mick spoke French very well for an Englishman, and at the time I spoke very little English. He was unpretentious, charming and had a great sense of humor.
>
> —BIANCA JAGGER, *Time*

coup de grâce (**koo** duh **grahs**) "finishing stroke"; a lethal blow or shot. A death blow administered to a wounded person to end the suffering, it probably originated in duels, with a dagger-thrust to the base of the skull. In the twentieth century it is typically a pistol shot to the head of an execution victim.

> I give this advice to those of my readers who are still at school. In every group there are boys whom it is the fashion to tease and bully; if you quickly spot them and join in, it will never occur to

anyone to tease and bully you. Foxes do not hunt stoats. But always defer to the original teasers, and hand your prey over to them for the *coup de grâce.*

—CYRIL CONNOLLY, "Where Engels Fears to Tread"

coup de main (**koo** duh **ma**^{n}) a bold, sudden thrust; a surprise attack.

It appears more like a line of march than a body intended for a *coup de main,* as there are with it bullocks and baggage of different kinds.

—DUKE OF WELLINGTON, *Dispatches*

coup de maître (**koo** duh **meh** truh) masterstroke.

coup de piston (**koo** duh pees **to**^{n}) a helping hand; an exercise of influence.

coup d'essai (**koo** deh **say**) "first attempt"; essay; experiment; trial.

coup d'état (**koo** day **tah**) "stroke of the state"; a seizure of power; a change of government by force. The term was first used to describe Cardinal Richelieu's (1585–1642) usurpation of power from Louis XIII.

coup de tête (**koo** duh **tet**) a brainstorm; an impulsive act.

coup de théâtre (**koo** duh tay **ah** truh) a sudden, dramatic gesture; a trick performance.

coup d'oeil (**koo** **doy**) quick glimpse; a general view.

I set off in pursuit of pots. Gazing into the windows of antique shops, I developed the *coup d'oeil* of the Great Napoleon . . . the ability to spot a rarity at ten paces.

—JULIAN CRITCHLEY, *The Times* (London)

coup manqué (**koo** mah^n **kay**) a failed attempt.

couture (**koo** **tür**) dressmaking; sewing; clothing fashion.

couturier (**koo** tü **ryay**) dressmaker; high-fashion designer.

craqueleur (krahk **luhr**) "crackle"; the small cracks that appear on the surface of a painting as it becomes brittle with age.

crème de la crème (**krehm** duh lah **krehm**) "cream of the cream"; the cream of society; the *élite*.

crêpe (krehp) a gauzy fabric embossed with wrinkles; a thin pancake.

crêpe de Chine (krehp duh **sheen**) a silken *crêpe* from China.

crépuscule (**kray** pü skül) twilight, the natural time of day for romance. See also, *cinq-à-sept*.

crève-coeur (krehv **kuhr**) heartbreak; bitter disappointment.

cri de coeur (kree duh **kuhr**) "cry of the heart"; heartfelt utterance; impassioned outcry.

> They break hearts, deals and chops, but these divas don't give a damn. . . . "If you have a vagina and a point of view," [Sharon] Stone has noted, "that's a deadly combination." No Hollywood heart is Stonier, of course, than that of Madonna, who deserves credit for coining its *cri de coeur*. "I have the same goal I've had since I was a girl," she said. "I want to rule the world."
>
> —SUSAN SCHINDEHETTE, *People*

cri de la conscience (kree duh lah ko^n **syah^{n}s**) voice of conscience.

crime passionnel (**kreem** pah syoh **nel**) crime of passion.

> Parisian juries tended to sympathize with perpetrators of the *crime passionnel*—and with women whose honor and respectability were threatened. A woman, overwhelmed by emotion, who killed to preserve her reputation . . . had hope for mercy; a woman who killed for political motives, who acted independently, could not.
>
> —JOAN DAHLGREN, *San Francisco Chronicle*

crise de coeur (kreez duh **kuhr**) "crisis of the heart"; an emotional upheaval.

crise de foi (kreez duh **fwah**) crisis of faith.

crise de foie (**kreez** duh **fwah**) "crisis of the liver"; a fashionable French complaint that may be cirrhosis, but usually isn't.

crise de la conscience (**kreez** duh lah ko^n **syo^{n}s**) crisis of conscience; moral dilemma.

crise de nerfs (**kreez** duh **nehr**) "crisis of nerves"; a brief nervous breakdown.

croissant (kwah **sah^n**) a crescent-shaped roll made with buttery dough.

croix de guerre (kwah duh **gehr**) "war cross"; a French military decoration for bravery.

croupier (kroo **pyay**) an attendant at a gaming table who handles bets.

cru (krü) "growth"; a vineyard or group of vineyards; a wine classification system which includes *premiers crus* (first growths), *grands crus* (great growths), and *crus exceptionnels* (exceptional growths).

crudités (krü dee **tay**) raw vegetables served as appetizers.

cuisine (kwee **zeen**) a distinctive style of preparing food; the food so prepared.

> *La cuisine française* is not one cuisine but a score, regional in origin, shading off into one another at their borders and all pulled together at Paris. Since certain of these cuisines are almost antithetical to certain others, the self-styled lover of *la cuisine française* without qualification is simply admitting that he has no taste at all.
>
> —A. J. LIEBLING, "The Modest Threshold"

cul de sac (kü duh **sahk**) "bottom of the bag"; a dead-end street.

> Two years ago, the Los Angeles Police Department launched Operation *Cul-de-Sac*, in which gang-infested streets are blocked to through traffic and police patrol the area on foot.
>
> —DEBORAH HASTINGS, *Chicago Tribune*

culte du moi (kült dü **mwah**) worship of the self; extreme selfishness.

cuvée (kü **vay**) the contents of a wine vat; a blend of various wines.

cy-près (**see** pray) "as possible"; a legal doctrine requiring the implementation of a testator's general intent when a will cannot be followed precisely.

d

d'accord (dah **kohr**) I'm in accord; agreed; okay.

Dada (dah dah) an early-twentieth-century European literary and artistic movement that rejected traditional cultural values and produced anarchic, absurd, incongruous works. The *Dada* credo, "Everything the artist spits is art," outraged contemporary critics, who labeled the movement "anti-art." *Dadaists* included Hans Arp (1887–1966), Marcel Duchamp (1887–1968), and Man Ray (1890–1976). According to legend the name *Dada*, which literally means "hobbyhorse," was chosen randomly by inserting a knife in a French dictionary.

dame de compagnie (**dahm** duh kohm pah **nyee**) lady's companion.

dame d'honneur (**dahm** doh **nuhr**) lady in waiting.

danse macabre (**dah^{n}s** mah **kah** bruh) "dance of death." The image of death as a dancing skeleton is an ancient one, dating at least as far back as the Etruscan civilization (circa 700 B.C.), and was common throughout Europe during the Middle Ages, appearing frequently in the churches of France and in the paintings of such artists as Hans Holbein.

> It's a never-ending *danse macabre*—perpetual midnight below the City of Lights. And it [the Paris Catacombs] attracts more than 100,000 curious visitors annually to a site once known as *Place d'Enfer*—The Place of Hell.
>
> —PETER MIKELBANK, *Washington Post*

Dauphin (doh **fa^n**) "dolphin"; the designation for the eldest son of a French king.

débâcle (day **bah** kluh) the breaking up of a frozen river, including the rush of ice and water that follows; hence a sudden breaking up or collapse; a stampede or rout; a total defeat; an abject failure. From *débâcler*, "to unbar."

de bonne grâce (duh bun **grahs**) with good grace; willingly; synonymous with *de bonne volonté*.

de bonne volonté (duh bun voh lo^n **tay**) with good grace; willingly; synonymous with *de bonne grâce*.

déclassé (**day** klah **say**) "declassed"; reduced in rank or status.

> Topless has gone Vegas. It's a Bugsy Siegel vision of its former self. What was once just *déclassé* raunch began to step up in style around 1988. Today the average upscale topless outlet will feature 20 to 30 women you wouldn't mind splicing genes with. And it comes with valet parking.
>
> —D. KEITH MANO, *Playboy*

déclassement (day klahs **mah**^{n}) loss of social status.

décolletage (day kohl **tahzh**) "low-cut neckline"; a dress with a low neckline exposing the neck and shoulders; partially bared breasts.

> Cher's favorite designer, Bob Mackie, ignored the new austerity, and his typically lavish show was a Hollywood production number for the cold-weather months, including a randy Santa Claus peering down a model's plunging *décolletage.*
>
> —MERYL GORDON, *The New Republic*

découpage (day koo **pahzh**) the technique of decorating with paper cutouts; a thing so decorated.

dégagé (day gah **zhay**) "disengaged"; free; uninhibited; relaxed.

> [Pierre] Cardin is careful to present himself as an artist as well as a moneymaker. With the *dégagé* demeanor of an aging *boulevardier*, Cardin slouches in a circular foam chair he designed back in the 1970s. "I have the most important name in the world," says Cardin in a monotone reminiscent of Truman Capote's.
>
> —RICHARD C. MORAIS, *Forbes*

d'égal à égal (day **gahl** ah ay **gahl**) "equal to equal"; equally.

dégôut (day **goo**) distaste; disgust.

de haut en bas (duh **oh** tah^n **bah**) "from high to low"; condescending.

> His style is provocatively *de haut en bas*; it is the style of a man who has spent a lifetime suffering fools ungladly.
>
> —JONATHAN RABAN of Gore Vidal in
> *The Los Angeles Times Book Review*

déjà vu (day zhah **vü**) "already seen"; the haunting sense of having lived an experience before.

> It's *déjà vu* all over again!
>
> —YOGI BERRA (attributed)

An Englishman understates, avoids the superlative, checks himself in compliments, alleging that in the French language one cannot speak without lying.
—RALPH WALDO EMERSON, *English Traits*, 1856

---

de mal en pis (duh **mahl** ah^n **pee**) from bad to worse; synonymous with *de pis en pis*.

démarche (**day** mahrsh) gait; step; a diplomatic overture signifying a new course of action or change of policy.

> After their meeting, the principals marched down the hall to the Oval Office to get Bush's assent to an ultimatum. No problem there. So on January 6, the Iraqi ambassador to the United Nations was handed an official *démarche*, giving Saddam forty-eight hours to disperse the batteries.
>
> —FRED BARNES, *The New Republic*

demi mondaine (**duh** mee mo^n **den**) a female inhabitant of the *demi monde* (which see), hence a disreputable woman.

> On the stage she's known as Camille (the woman of the camellias) but in the world of opera she's Violetta Valery, "la traviata" (the lost one), a butterfly who dwells on the fringes of high society and lives only for pleasure. Verdi's beloved 1853 opera tells the

story of the 11th-hour romance that turns this jaded *demi mondaine* into a passionate if doomed lover.

—LAWRENCE BOMMER, *Chicago Tribune*

demi monde (**duh** mee **moⁿd**) "half-world"; the fringes of society; the underworld.

demitasse (deh mee **tahss**) "half-cup"; a small coffee cup.

demi-vierge (**duh** mee vee **yehrzh**) "half-virgin"; a woman who is technically a virgin but is not sexually inexperienced.

It was in her second winter at Wragby her father said to her: "I hope, Connie, you won't let circumstances force you into being a *demi-vierge*."
"A *demi-vierge*!" replied Connie vaguely. "Why? Why not?"
"Unless you like it, of course!" said her father hastily. To Clifford he said the same, when the two men were alone: "I'm afraid it doesn't quite suit Connie to be a *demi-vierge*."
"A half-virgin!" replied Clifford, translating the phrase to be sure of it.
He thought for a moment, then flushed very red. He was angry and offended.
"In what way doesn't it suit her?" he asked stiffly.
"She's getting thin . . . angular. It's not her style. She's not the pilchard sort of little slip of a girl, she's a bonny Scotch trout."

—D. H. LAWRENCE, *Lady Chatterley's Lover*

démodé (**day** moh **day**) outmoded; old-fashioned.

He paused, and Laura felt herself blushing. Partly because she detested so *démodé* and unsuitable a manifestation of her feelings, and partly from pure nervousness, she dashed into speech.

—E. M. DELAFIELD, *The Way Things Are*

(le) démon de midi ([luh] day **moⁿ** duh mee dee) "(the) demon at noon"; the resurgence of sexual desire in middle age; mid-life crisis.

dénouement (**day** noo **mahⁿ**) literally, "action of untying" (from *dénouer*, "to untie, undo"); the unraveling or final resolution of a plot; the upshot or outcome of any complicated situation or series of events.

(le) démon de midi

Many of the stories are written round, rather than toward, their *dénouements*.

—*Times Literary Supplement*

de`nouveau (**duh** noo **voh**) anew.

département (**day** pahrt **mah**^{n}) the largest administrative division of the French government; a province.

de par le roi (duh **pahr** luh **rwah**) in the name of the king.

dépaysé (**day** pay ee **zay**) out of one's natural element; far from home; homesick.

dépêche (day **pesh**) dispatch; message.

de pied en cap (duh **pyay** ah^n **kahp**) from head to foot.

de pis en pis (duh pee zah^n **pee**) from bad to worse (synonymous with *de mal en pis*).

déplacé (**day** plah **say**) displaced; ill-timed.

de prix (duh **pree**) valuable; expensive.

déprimé (**day** pree **may**) depressed; discouraged; low; flat.

déraciné (**day** rah see **nay**) uprooted; separated from one's natural element.

> As background we get, in snippets, the autobiography of Michael Straight. For starters, he was rich and *déraciné*, growing up an expatriate in a British upper-class milieu. To this cosmopolitan experience he attributes his later susceptibility to the wiles of Burgess, Blunt, and the other Apostles at Cambridge.
>
> —JOHN P. ROCHE, *National Review*

dérangé (**day** rah^n **zhay**) disturbed; upset; ruffled; in disorder.

de règle (duh **rehg** luh) required by law or convention.

de rigueur (duh ree **guhr**) required by fashion or custom; absolutely necessary; compulsory.

> Amenities such as gymnasiums and health centers are *de rigueur* in the growing ranks of Southern Baptist mega-churches that now number more than 50.
>
> —JAMES C. HEFLEY, *Saturday Evening Post*

dernier cri (**dehr** nyay **kree**) "the last cry"; the last word; the latest style.

> Today, few beagles or schnauzers would be caught dead in a suburban mall without a dog sweater. According to a *New York Times* report on what well-dressed dogs are wearing in the Big Apple, the *dernier cri* in canine couture [is] a cashmere scarf tied ever so *à la Parisienne* round Rover's neck.
>
> —RICHARD WOLKOMIR, *Smithsonian*

derrière (deh **ryehr**) buttocks. According to *A Dictionary of Euphemisms & Other Doubletalk* by Hugh Rawson, the first example of the use of *derrière* as an English euphemism dates to 1747: "Naturally, being British, it has to do with spanking: '*S'il fait le fier*. I shall give him several spanks upon his *derrière*."

désagrément (**day** zah gray **mah**ⁿ) trouble; unpleasantness; embarrassment.

déshabillé (day zah bee **yay**) in a state of undress; in a *negligé*; sloppily dressed.

> When Rita Hayworth posed kneeling on a bed, *en déshabillé* to make the 1941 poster that every GI hung over his bunk, she was 22.
>
> —ERIC LEVIN, *People*

désolé (day soh **lay**) "desolate"; disconsolate.

détente (day **tah**ⁿt) "loosening"; an easing of tension between governments. According to *Fighting Words* by Christine Ammer, the term originally referred to the slackening of pressure on a gun's trigger, which was "detained" in order to fire the gun. It has been used figuratively in English since about 1910, to describe the relief of tension between nations through diplomatic means.

de trop (duh **troh**) excessive, superfluous.

> The Procope was refurbished with a vengeance in 1988—Pompeian red walls, 18th-century oval portraits, crystal chandeliers, flintlock pistols and, for the waiters, quasi-revolutionary uniforms. Also a tinkly piano. If that all seems something that even Napoleon might call *de trop*, the food is generally good (Michelin recommends it), and the oysters are a joy.
>
> —OTTO FRIEDRICH, *Time*

diablerie (dyah bluh **ree**) devilry; wanton mischief; graphic representations of the satanic.

> Debra Winger has neither Claire Bloom's loveliness nor Jane Alexander's ironic *hauteur*, but she has a wonderfully idiosyncratic bounciness—almost a tomboyish *diablerie*.
>
> —JOHN SIMON, *National Review*

diabolique (dyah boh **leek**) diabolical; devilish.

difficile (dee fee **seel**) hard; difficult to deal with; demanding; troublesome.

> As the *Figaro* said the next day, Rouen audiences were known to be "*très difficiles*": conscious of being thought provincial, they insisted on "being shown." (Indeed, in nineteenth-century French theatrical circles the expression "All aboard for Rouen" signified expectation of the worst.)
>
> —FRANCIS STEEGMULLER, "*Salammbô*: The Career of an Opera"

diplomate de carrière (**dee** ploh maht duh kah **ryehr**) career diplomat (as opposed to a political appointee).

diplomatie (dee **ploh** mah **tee**) diplomacy.

dirigisme (dee ree **zheesm**) state economic planning and control, the opposite of *laissez-faire*.

> The two existing orthodox business structures were complete non-starters: U.S. conventional management—business by committee—crippled any initiative that existed at IBM and the rest of the computer establishment; Japanese robotic *dirigisme*, which had destroyed the Western manufacturing base, was simply unable to harness the anarchic brains of the pizza-guzzling, anorak-wearing, science-fiction addict constituency of computer programmers.
>
> —RICHARD LANDER, *The Independent*

diseur/diseuse (dee **zuhr**/dee **zuhz**) a dramatic monologist.

> She had been quite famous in her youth. . . . She had won a reputation as a *diseuse* and had appeared regularly in intimate revues until these things went out of style.
>
> —ANITA BROOKNER, *Brief Lives*

distingué (dees ta^n **gay**) distinguished.

distrait (dee **stray**) distracted; absentminded.

> Unfortunately [Andie] MacDowell, who had a helium-headed charm in *Sex, Lies, and Videotape*, seems to have lost it here. *Distrait* and underpowered, she looks as if she is thinking of another movie.
>
> —NIGEL ANDREWS, *Financial Times* (London)

divertissement (dee **vehr** tees **mah**ⁿ) diversion; amusement; a brief entertainment; a short ballet or other performance presented *entr'acte* (which see) of an opera or play; an entire program of such brief performances.

donnée (doh **nay**) that which is given; a known quantity; the theme or motif of a story.

doré (doh **ray**) golden.

douane (doo **ahn**) custom house; customs.

douanier (doo ah **nyay**) customs officer.

douceur de vivre (doo **suhr** duh **veev** ruh) the pleasures of the good life.

> Brillat-Savarin was no Talleyrand as an observer of American manners, apart from his delight in fresh young ladies (another of his tastes) and turkey shoots—reminding us that Thanksgiving turkeys were worth eating when shot on the wing in the Connecticut woods. But like so many returned exiles, his lost *douceur de vivre* infused his autobiography, sensuous as Colette's.
>
> —CHRISTOPHER DRIVER, *The Guardian*

double entendre (**doo** bluh ahⁿ **tah**ⁿ druh) "double meaning"; having two meanings, one of which is *risqué* (which see); ambiguously sexual.

> "Electronics is a strange thing," he said with that authoritative manner used by people who can understand the lyrics of rock 'n' roll songs when dealing with people who remember when you could not only hear a Lorenz Hart lyric on the radio but also grasp the *double entendre* in every word of it.
>
> —RUSSELL BAKER, *New York Times*

doyen (dwah **ya**ⁿ) the senior member of a group or profession. The feminine form is *doyenne* (dwah **yehn**).

draperie mouillée (drah **pree** moo **yay**) "wet draperie"; clinging draperie in painting or sculpture that reveals the underlying form.

droit de seigneur (**drwah** duh sehn **yuhr**) "right of the lord." It was the prerogative of a medieval feudal lord to deflower the bride of his vassal on their wedding night. Now the term refers derisively to someone who arrogantly asserts power.

The communications industry has moved on. Broadcasting has broken the newspaper's monopoly on political access. More assertive journalism has eroded the *droit de seigneur* of ownership; for better or worse, politicians *fête* editors and columnists these days. Proprietors pontificate: it is expected of them. But the days of their greatness are over.

—SIMON JENKINS, *Sunday Times* (London)

(le) droit du plus fort **([luh] drwaht** dü plü **fohr)** "(the) right of the stronger"; might makes right.

droit naturel **(drwah** nah tü **rel)** the natural rights of man.

drôle **(drohl)** droll; comic.

du meilleur rang **(dü may** yuhr **rah^n)** of the highest rank; aristocratic.

d'un certain âge **(du^n** sehr ten **nahzh)** "of a certain age"; a euphemism for "middle-aged."

Limousines belong on the palm-lined avenues of Beverly Hills, not on the sunless streets of London. And it is not every day that a *femme d'un certain âge* sweeps through the Palm Court clad entirely in black from her palazzo pants, to sweeping shades and the Lana Turner turban around her head. At 57, Joan Collins looks sensational.

—ALICE RAWSTHORN, *Financial Times* (London)

eau de vie (oh duh **vee**) "water of life," i.e., cheap brandy.

éclat (ay **klah**) great brilliance; conspicuous success or acclamation.

écrasez l'infâme (ay krah **zay** la^n **fahm**) "Wipe out the infamous thing"; crush the abomination. The battle cry of the French philosopher, poet, and dramatist Voltaire (François-Marie Arouet, 1694–1778), referring variously to the Catholic Church, the *ancien régime* (which see), or whatever else incurred his displeasure.

écritoire (eh kree **twahr**) writing desk.

élan (ay **lah**^{n}) flair; spirit; enthusiasm.

> *Sliver* (R) is a peep show that is all peep and not much of a show; another lurid potboiler from screenwriter Joe Eszterhas (*Jagged Edge, Basic Instinct*), who slaps together a mystery with the *élan* of a bricklayer.
>
> —STEVE PERSALL, *St. Petersburg Times*

élan vital (ay **lah**^{n} vee **tahl**) "life force"; the name of the philosopher Henri Bergson's (1859–1941) metaphysical theory that all living things possess an enduring force which accounts for the creative evolution of life. *Élan vital*, "the idea with a sword," was also the basis of the aggressive French military doctrine following the Franco-Prussian War (1870–71).

> Depression so destroys the components of the mind-body relationship that creativity is beyond question. You have no *élan vital*, none of the things that make creativity possible.
>
> —WILLIAM STYRON

embarras de richesses (ahm bah **rah** duh ree **shess**) "embarrassment of riches"; overwhelming abundance.

Altogether, within its choice and compacted range, the Pushkin [Museum] affords an irresistible *embarras de richesses*, to which I succumbed three times.

—WILLIAM PACKER, *Financial Times* (London)

embarras du choix (ahm bah **rah** dü **shwah**) embarrassing variety of choice.

embourgeoisement (ahm boor zhwahz **mah**[n]) the gradual conversion to *bourgeois* values.

One thing that has happened to the working class is *embourgeoisement*. They've got their cars and their color TVs, and they're coming to think that they're more middle class than working class."

—BRIAN FLANAGAN, *Business Week*

émigré (**ay** mee **gray**) "emigrant"; exile; the term was particularly applied to the royalists and aristocrats who fled France during the Revolution.

éminence grise (**ay** mee nah[n]s **greez**) "gray cardinal"; gray eminence; the power behind the throne. The term originally referred to Joseph le Clerc du Tremblay (1577–1638) also known as Père Joseph, the confessor and political adviser to Cardinal Richelieu (1585–1642), minister to Louis XIII.

en bloc (ah[n] **blohk**) in a mass; as a whole; wholesale.

enceinte (ah[n] sa[n]t) pregnant.

Sue Halpern was two months away from motherhood when she visited the Caribbean. She felt so "blissed out" snorkeling *enceinte* that she decided to give birth in an immersion tub.

—THOMAS J. WALLACE, *Condé Nast Traveler*

endimanché (ah[n] dee mah[n] **shay**) dressed in one's "Sunday best."

en effet (ah[n] nay **fay**) in fact; actually; indeed.

en famille (ah[n] fah **mee**) in or with one's family; at home.

Whether the angels play only Bach in praising God I am not quite sure; I am sure, however, that *en famille* they play only Mozart.

—KARL BARTH

enfant chéri (ah^n fah^n shay ree) favored child.

enfants perdus (ah^n fah^n pehr dü) "lost children"; soldiers sent on a suicidal mission.

enfant terrible (ah^n fah^n tay ree bluh) "terrible child"; a precocious, unruly child; an impetuous, embarrassing person. Extremely talented young artists, writers, and film directors have been particularly subject to this designation (Oscar Wilde, Orson Welles, and Steven Spielberg are classic examples), but perhaps one need not be an *enfant* to be an *enfant terrible*:

> At 66, [Gore] Vidal appears to be just coming to his full dimensions as an *enfant terrible*.
>
> —JONATHAN RABAN, *Los Angeles Times Book Review*

en fin (ah^n fa^n) in conclusion; in summary; in a word.

engagé (ah^n gah zhay) "engaged"; politically active; committed. From the Old French *engagier*, "to pledge."

en grand seigneur (ah^n grah^{n}d say nyuhr) in grand style.

en grande tenue (ah^n grah^{n}d tuh nü) in full dress uniform.

> There was no bemedalment in evidence at Protocol Chief Joseph Verner Reed's farewell reception Thursday night at Blair House. No *soirée en grande tenue* this, just bussing and bearhugs for 250 friends arriving to see him off to his new post as U.N. representative.
>
> —KEVIN CHAFFEE, *Washington Times*

en grande toilette (ah^n grah^{n}d twah let) in full dress. Roughly synonymous with *en grande tenue*.

> The dancers are further lumbered with the most hideous and capricious clothes I have seen on the dance stage this year—some of the men in tartan trews with mini-kilts; the women given

dresses that make them look like Soviet lady truck drivers *en grande toilette.*

—CLEMENT CRISP, *Financial Times* (London)

en guerre (ah^n **gehr**) at war; in opposition.

en masse (ah^n **mahss**) as a whole; in a group.

en ménage (ah^n may **nahzh**) an unmarried couple living as husband and wife.

ennui (ah^n **nwee**) boredom; world-weariness.

Ennui, felt on the proper occasions, is a sign of intelligence.

—CLIFTON FADIMAN, *Reading I've Liked*

ennuyé (ah^n nwee yay) bored; world-weary; annoyed.

en pantoufles (ah^n **pah^n** too fluh) in slippers; informal; relaxed.

en papillotes (ah^n pah pee **yoht**) "in paper"; a dish cooked or served wrapped in parchment paper; in curl papers; in a state of undress (i.e., as naked as a lamb chop with those little paper booties on it).

en passant (ah^n **pah** sah^n) "in passing"; incidentally; in chess, the lateral capture of a pawn by a pawn.

en pension (ah^n pah^n **syo^n**) in a boardinghouse.

en plein (ah^n **plai^n**) fully; completely; in roulette, a bet on a single number.

en plein air (ah^n plai^n **nehr**) in the open air.

en plein jour (ah^n plai^n **zhoor**) in broad daylight.

en poste (ah^n **pohst**) in a (diplomatic) post.

en prise (ah^n **preez**) in chess, a piece subject to immediate capture, and hence anything in jeopardy.

Beginning with the Soweto school riots in June, 1976, evidence has been mounting that the African majority, having lost patience at being excluded from the political system, is turning to more forceful methods of fighting for its rights. With Portuguese colonialism driven out of Africa at last, and Rhodesia *en prise*, it feels its time has come.

—*The Economist*

en rapport (ah^n rah **pohr**) in harmony; in agreement.

en règle (ah^n **reh** gluh) in order; in proper form.

en retraite (ah^n ruh **tret**) in retreat; in retirement.

en revanche (ah^n ruh **vah^{n}sh**) in return; in retaliation; return match.

en route (ah^n **root**) on the way.

ensemble (ah^n **sahm** bluh) "together"; a small musical or theatrical group; a complete costume (including accessories).

en suite (ah^n **sweet**) in company; in a series; in succession; in agreement. Also, a set of rooms opening onto one another.

> "I've always wanted an *en suite* bathroom," she would say to visitors, to her friends on the phone, to, he wouldn't be surprised, tradesmen on the doorstep or strangers she accosted in the street. You would think *en suite* was the most beautiful phrase in any language, the lengths Marjorie went to put it into her conversation. If they made a perfume called *En suite*, she would wear it.
>
> —DAVID LODGE, *Nice Work*

entente (ah^n **tah^{n}t**) understanding; agreement.

entente cordiale (ah^n **tah^{n}t** kohr **dyahl**) a "cordial understanding" between nations; an international agreement not amounting to a formal alliance. The term has been most prominently applied to relations between the French and British, first in 1844 when the French statesman François Guizot (1787–1874) achieved a "cordial understanding" with Lord Aberdeen (1847–1934), and then in 1904, following a goodwill visit to Paris by King Edward VII (1841–1910).

entr'acte (ah^n **trahkt**) "between acts"; the interval between the acts of a play; interlude.

en train (ah^n **tra^n**) in progress.

entrechat (ah^n truh **shah**) a ballet leap in which the legs are rapidly crossed and uncrossed in midair.

entre deux âges (ah^n truh duh **zahzh**) "between two ages"; middle-aged.

entre deux guerres (ah^n truh duh **gehr**) "between two wars"; the period from 1918 to 1939.

Jack would be a gentleman if he could speak French.
— JOHN HEYWOOD, *Proverbs*, 1546

---

entrée (ah^n **tray**) right of admission; the main course of a meal.

entremets (ah^n truh **may**) side dish.

entre nous (ah^n truh **noo**) "between us"; confidentially.

Conspiracy theories have gotten a bad name lately. The very word "conspiracy" evokes skepticism, though it shouldn't, since there are plenty of sneaky people in this world and they manage to find each other fairly often. And we're well aware of the gap in politics between the way people talk in front of a camera and the way they talk *entre nous*.

— JOSEPH SOBRAN, *National Review*

entrepôt (ah^n truh **poh**) warehouse; distribution depot.

en voyage (ah^n vwah **yahzh**) on a trip; traveling.

envoyé (ah^n vwah **yay**) envoy; ambassador.

épater le bourgeois (ay pah **tay** luh boor **zhwah**) "rattle the middle class"; flout convention; confound the Philistines; shock the squares by some extreme behavior, such as dyeing your hair green (as Baudelaire is reputed to have done on one occasion).

> [Sandra] Bernhard's whole kitschy persona . . . is all about exaggerated emotion acted out in abjection and *épatering the bourgeois*, a rebellion against suburbia that is itself very much a product of the subdivisions.
>
> —JULIE PHILLIPS, *Voice Literary Supplement*

épaulette (**ay** poh **let**) a shoulder ornament, particularly a fringed strap, formerly worn on military uniforms.

épée (ay **pay**) sword.

épergne (ay **pehr** nyuh) a decorative centerpiece.

> A great, hideous, candlesticklike affair that stood in the middle of Victorian dinner tables and occasionally held flowers or food but was mainly there to look impressive.
>
> —DANIEL POOL, *What Jane Austen Ate and Dickens Knew*

esprit de corps (es **pree** duh **kohr**) group spirit or loyalty.

> It is impossible not to personify a ship; everybody does, in everything they say:—she behaves well; she minds her rudder; she swims like a duck; she runs her nose into the water; she looks into a port. Then that wonderful *esprit de corps*, by which we adopt into our self-love everything we touch, makes us all champions of her sailing qualities.
>
> —RALPH WALDO EMERSON, *English Traits*

esprit de l'escalier (es **pree** duh les kahl **yay**) "wit of the staircase"; a witty remark thought of too late.

> There really ought to be an expression to convey the opposite of *esprit de l'escalier*. This would suggest not a clever remark that occurs to one after the opportunity to make it is lost, but a clever remark which is planned but never made when the opportunity arises.
>
> —OLIVER PRITCHETT, *Sunday Telegraph* (London)

esprit de notaire (es **pree** duh noh **tehr**) the "soul of a lawyer"; the tendency to be legalistic, to split hairs.

esprit de l'escalier

esprit fort (es pree fohr) a freethinker.

esprit gaulois (es pree gohl wah) Gallic wit.

esprit libre (es pree lee bruh) free spirit.

esprit présent (es pree pray sah[n]) quick mind; ready wit.

estaminet (es tah mee nay) wine shop; pub.

étagère (ay tah zhehr) a piece of furniture with open shelves for displaying *objets*. From the Old French *estagière*, "scaffold."

étoile (ay twahl) star; a design in the shape of a star; an intersection with streets converging on a single point.

étude (ay tüd) "study"; a composition designed to improve the musician's technique, e.g., finger exercises such as Chopin's *Études*.

exercice de style (eks ehr sees duh steel) a work intended as a technical exercise and not as a serious work of art.

The veteran Alfredo Kraus makes his Romeo a series of dedicated *exercices de style* (though his refined clarity exposes some foreign vowels).

—DAVID MURRAY, *Financial Times* (London)

expéditeur (eks **pay** dee tuhr) sender; dispatcher.

explication de texte (eks plee kah **syo**^{n} duh **tekst**) a thorough analysis of the style and content of a literary work.

extrados (eks **trah** doh) the outer surface of an arch or vault.

f

fabliau (fah blee **oh**) a medieval, often ribald tale in Old French.

façon (fah **so**ⁿ) fashion; style; manner.

façon de parler (fah **so**ⁿ duh pahr **lay**) "manner of speaking"; figure of speech.

fainéant (fay nay **ah**ⁿ) lazy; idle; slothful; an idler; a sluggard. This is a French example of a portmanteau word, combining the verb *faire* (to do) with the archaic *néant* (nothing).

faire sans dire (fehr sah ⁿ **deer**) to do without speaking; to act quietly but effectively.

fait accompli (**fay** tah kohm **plee**) "accomplished fact"; a thing done.

faites vos jeux (**feht** voh zhuh) "make your sport"; place your bets (at roulette).

faits divers (**feht** dee **vehr**) "news in brief"; short news items.

fantaisiste (fah ⁿ tay **zeest**) a writer or painter whose work is whimsical or fantastical.

farceur (fahr **suhr**) joker; clown; buffoon; one who writes or performs in farces.

> We have rediscovered that Chekhov the lyrical poet of decay is usually accompanied by another Chekhov: the inspired *farceur*, the transcendental joker who is the missing link between Gogol and Nabokov.
>
> —JOHN PETER, *Sunday Times* (London)

farouche (fah **roosh**) sullen; unsociable; savage.

I am old enough to remember the furor when [Nureyev] defected to the West in 1961. He was the first of the ballet defectors, and he seemed unbelievably exotic—not just a Russian, but a Tartar, whatever that was. He could jump further and higher than anyone else; he was *farouche* and temperamental; above all, he was beautiful.

—LYNN BARBER, *The Independent*

faute (foht) fault; error; mistake; lack.

faute de mieux (foht duh **myuh**) for want of something better.

(les) Fauves ([lay] **fohv**) "(the) wild beasts"; the pejorative applied by a now forgotten critic to an early-twentieth-century school of painting characterized by decorative simplicity and brilliant color. Among *les Fauves* were Matisse, Dufy, Rouault, and Vlaminck.

faux amis (foh zah **mee**) "false friends"; two words from different languages which seem to have the same meaning but do not, i.e., "deceptive cognates." Thus, in French a *baladeur* is a stroller, not a singer, *petulant* means "lively," *destitution* means "dismissal," and a *jerk* is a good dancer.

faux brave (**foh** brahv) "false bravery"; bravado; swagger.

faux bonhomme (**foh** boh **nohm**) a falsely good-natured man; one who feigns cordiality.

faux dévot (**foh** day **voh**) "falsely devout"; a pious hypocrite.

faux ménage (**foh** may **nahzh**) an ill-suited marriage; a union of incompatibles; an odd couple.

faux naïf (**foh** nai **eef**) one who feigns credulity or artlessness.

What place in the post-mod pantheon do you assign a fellow who's as talented as he is humorless, who has an ear that just won't quit to go with a wit that just won't start, who's as gifted a self-producer as he is a *poseur*? Do you dismiss him as a *faux naïf* or laud him as an idiot savant?

—CHRIS WILLMAN, "Lenny Kravitz, How Retro Can You Go,"
Los Angeles Times

faux pas (foh **pah**) "false step"; social blunder; breach of etiquette.

> Women's fashion *faux pas* often come from trying too hard; men's from not trying at all.
>
> —*Glamour Magazine*

femme de chambre (**fahm** duh **shahm** bruh) a lady's maid; chambermaid.

femme du monde (**fahm** dü **mo**^{n}**d**) "woman of the world"; sophisticated woman; society woman.

> French dress designers, hairdressers, and cooks are admitted to be unbeatable, but they lose their eye, their hand, their skill after a few years in England or America. Why? Because they are no longer under the disciplinary control of *les femmes du monde*— that is to say, of a very few rich, ruthless, and savagely energetic women who know what they want and never spare anybody's feelings in their determination to get it.
>
> —NANCY MITFORD, "Chic—English, French and American"

femme fatale (**fahm** fah **tahl**) "deadly woman"; a woman who leads men to disaster; a vamp; an enchantress.

> We've had a whole series of *femme fatale* movies—*Fatal Attraction* and *Basic Instinct* and *The Hand that Rocks the Cradle* and this recent Madonna movie—and people keep going to these movies and making them big box office hits and the feminists keep objecting to them. But the truth is these are examples of how women dominate. . . . Amy Fisher is a *femme fatale* and a corrective to the distortions of things like the weepy scenarios of victimology.
>
> —CAMILLE PAGLIA, *Newsday*

femme incomprise (**fahm** a^n kohm **preez**) a misunderstood or unappreciated woman.

femme savante (**fahm** sah **vah**^{n}**t**) intellectual woman; learned woman; "bluestocking"; from *Les Femmes Savantes* (1672), a comedy by Molière.

fête (**feht**) festival; celebration; to celebrate; to honor.

fête champêtre (**feht** shah^n **peh** truh) outdoor festival; a large garden party; a style of bucolic painting practiced by Watteau (1684–1721) also known as *fête galante.*

fête galante (**feht** gah **lah^{n}t**) see *fête champêtre.*

feu de joie (**fuh** duh **zhwah**) "fire of joy"; a military salute with rifles or cannons.

feuilleton (**foy** eh **to^n**) a literary newspaper column; a serial novel.

feux d'artifice (**fuh** dahr tee **fees**) fireworks.

> Normally, there would have been *feux d'artifice* shooting up from the field behind the war memorial. This year, because of the drought, fireworks are forbidden. But it was a good *fête.* And did you see how the postman danced?
>
> —PETER MAYLE, *Toujours Provence*

fille de chambre (fee duh **shahm** bruh) lady's maid.

fille de joie (fee duh **zhwah**) "daughter of joy"; prostitute.

fille publique (fee püb **leek**) prostitute.

film noir (film **nwahr**) "black film"; the label applied to Hollywood movies made in the late forties and early fifties characterized by shadowy lighting and a cynical point of view. Prominent examples of the genre include *The Maltese Falcon* (1941), *This Gun for Hire* (1942), *The Killers* (1946), and *White Heat* (1949).

> The Safe Driving School was located on the second floor of a rinky-dink building on a heavily trafficked street in a bad part of town. It could have been the setting for a *film noir.*
>
> —ANDREI CODRESCU, *Road Scholar*

fils (fees) "son"; used after a name to distinguish son from father when they have the same name, as in "Alexandre Dumas, *fils.*"

fils à papa (fees ah pah **pah**) "papa's boy"; a rich man's son; playboy.

fin (fa^n) end; finish.

fin de siècle (fa^n duh see ehk luh) "end of century"; the decadent era at the close of the nineteenth century.

> Certain expressions can be rendered only in French. *Esprit de corps. Joie de vivre. Cherchez la femme. Croissant.* They don't really work in translation. And that is true of *fin de siècle.* "End of the century" sounds flat and clunky. It doesn't carry the suggestion conveyed by the original of hectic decay and a sort of perfumed dying fall.
>
> —HENRY GRUNWALD, *Time*

fin de race (fa^n duh rahss) "end of breed"; decadent aristocrats.

flacon (flah ko^n) flask; vial.

flâneur (flah nuhr) layabout; idler.

flèche (flesh) arrow; spire.

fléchette (flay shet) dart.

Flèche d'Or (flesh dohr) "Golden Arrow"; a fast train between London and Paris that ceased operating in the late 1960s.

foie gras (fwah grah) enriched goose or duck liver produced by force-feeding the bird.

folie à deux (foh lee ah duh) "madness for two"; mutual delusion.

folie de grandeur (foh lee duh grah^n duhr) delusions of grandeur; megalomania.

> Paul McCartney's massive *folie de grandeur,* the semi-autobiographical *Liverpool Oratorio* . . . cruelly exposed the pretensions of a man who, as he freely admitted at the time, cannot write music and does not feel you need to be able to when "composing" for the Liverpool Philharmonic.
>
> —ROBERT SANDALL, *Sunday Times* (London)

force de dissuasion (fors duh dee swah zyo^n) the current official term for the French long-range nuclear striking force.

force de frappe (**fors** duh **frahp**) "strike force"; the former official term for the French long-range nuclear striking force.

force majeure (**fors** mah **zhuhr**) irresistible force; a clause that excuses performance of a contractual duty made impossible by an "act of God."

formidable! (fohr me **dah** bluh) tremendous!; splendid!; wonderful!

fou (foo) mad; crazy; insane.

foulard (foo **lahr**) a silken fabric used for neckties; a necktie or handkerchief of *foulard*.

franc-tireur (**frah**^{n} teeh **ruhr**) "freeshooter"; sniper. The plural, *francs-tireurs*, refers to French paramilitary units formed from rifle clubs that served in the Franco-Prussian war of 1870–71.

fraude pieuse (frohd pyuhz) pious deceit.

frère (frehr) brother; friar.

frisson (free **so**^{n}) shiver; shudder; a brief but intense thrill. From the Old French *friçon*, "a trembling."

> The trouble this year with the awards, whose name was supposedly "Oscar Celebrates Women and the Movies," was that the oblique signals and hidden references were too simplified and the over-all treatment was too numb, or too dumb. There was no *frisson*, no scandal, as a conscious, sly thread through the show.
>
> —HAROLD BRODKEY, *The New Yorker*

frondeur (fro^n **duhr**) a faultfinder; a malcontent; from the Fronde, an opposition political faction during the minority of Louis XIV.

> In 1937, Nazi chiefs Heinrich Himmler and Joachim von Ribbentrop entertained the Duke of Windsor there. It was a regular favourite of the chief of German military intelligence, Admiral Wilhelm Canaris. But Horchers was never Nazi. Most of the anti-Nazi *frondeurs* ate there and the Gestapo was not welcome.
>
> —GILES MACDONOGH, *Financial Times* (London)

frou-frou (froo-froo) the rustle of a silk dress; ribbons 'n' ruffles.

The Colette room, with all its ruffles, frills and porcelain cats, was a little too *frou-frou* for my liking, but I'm sure more than a few couples have romantic memories of it.

—DAWN HANNA, *Vancouver Sun*

fruit(s) de mer (frwee duh mehr) "fruit of the sea"; seafood.

Franglais
~

The language of Molière and Descartes, Rimbaud and Verlaine, has contributed countless loanwords to the English language by the process of acculturation over centuries. On the other hand English, especially American English, has inundated the French language on a wave of postwar hegemony. It has infused French not only with countless technical terms, but also with Franglais, a hybrid of English and French. America has given France not only Levi's and Jerry Lewis, but also *le drug store, le stress*, and *les chicken nuggets*.

Franglais, a portmanteau combination of *Français* and *Anglais*, can be traced at least as far back as 1833, with the naming of the exclusive *Le Jockey Club* (membership in which was a sign of Swann's high social status in Proust's *A la recherche du temps perdu*). Franglais has been a useful linguistic tool for Francophones ever since, largely because the formalistic French language has adapted little to a world increasingly influenced by American pop culture.

American English is fashionable in France, especially among young Parisians, who love the word *super*; it is indispensable in technical matters, because much of the world's technology emanates from the United States; and it is gaining favor with Eurocrats, having supplanted French as the working language of the European Community (where it is referred to by supporters as *Eurospeak* and by detractors as *Desperanto*).

But there is also strong resistance to Franglais. In 1964 René Etiemble, a professor of comparative literature at the Sorbonne, published *Parlez-Vous Franglais?*, a dictionary of French substitutes for Americanisms. Etiemble called for severe fines against *Américanolâtres*, "America worshipers." His rationale: "The French language is a treasure. To violate it is a crime. Persons were shot during the war for treason. They should be punished for degrading the

[French] language." Etiemble is in a hallowed tradition. As far back as 1757, Forgeret de Monbron published *Préservatif contre l'anglomanie,* a denunciation of the influx of English words into French.

Nor have the French been receptive to American pop culture. The Coca-Cola Company's attempt to build a bottling plant in France in the late 1940s created a furor, the Paris Opera was once fined for using English in a program, and the French government has tried to limit the number of American programs on French television ("Wheel of Fortune"—*La Roue de la Fortune*—is one of the most popular shows). Jack Lang, when he was the French minister of culture, rallied the attack against American influence in a 1982 speech in which he denounced American "cultural imperialism."

EuroDisney was thus greeted with disdain when it opened near Paris in the spring of 1992. Labor unions staged protests, a French expert on fairy tales charged that Disney "simplifies folklore and makes it banal," and a Parisian theater director called it a "cultural Chernobyl." (It has reportedly lost close to a billion dollars.) And *Jurassic Park*'s dinosaurs were loudly assailed in France as creatures of a predatory American pop culture.

It is in this climate that the Académie Française, operating on the principle that "what is not clear is not French," officially bans Franglais words (all of which arbitrarily take the masculine pronoun) and decrees their replacement with tortured new constructions. Under this Frenchification program, *le weekend* becomes *fin de semaine, le fast food* becomes *le prêt-à-manger, brainstorming* becomes *remueméninges* ("brain-mixing"), *jumbo jet* becomes *avion grosporteur,* and *le airbag* becomes *coussin gonflable de protection. Marketing* is replaced by *mercatique, Jeep*—a brand name with no French equivalent—must be spelled *Jipe,* and *le Walkman* (not even an English word but rather a Japanese marketer's conception of an Americanism) shall henceforth be *le baladeur* (wanderer).

American computer terms such as "hardware," "software," "keyboard," and "buffer" have passed unchanged into the French lexicon, much to the distress of President François Mitterrand. On a visit to Silicon Valley in 1984, he asked Steven Jobs, the cofounder of Apple Computer, why there was so little French software in use outside France. Jobs replied, "The problem is, it's written in French. You can't sell it." Nevertheless, in a speech before the Académie Française in 1986, Mitterrand stubbornly warned, "Either the French language learns to master computer technology, or in a few years it ceases to be one of the great means of communication in the world." Mitterrand then asked rhetorically, "Must we translate into English the orders that we give machines?" *Le software* thus becomes *le logiciel*. The substitute for "buffer"? *Mémoire tampon*.

American business terms are also under attack: *les blue chips, les debt equity swaps,* and *le venture capital* are to be replaced by *valeur de premier ordre, échange de créances contre actifs,* and *capital-risque. Capital-risque?* No wonder the French public has rejected the fiat vocabulary.

The French linguistic inquisition has many tentacles. In addition to the Académie Française, which publishes the official French dictionary, the Association of Users of the French Language enforces compliance with a 1975 law requiring French businesses to use French instead of English; the General Commissariat of the French Language periodically issues blacklists of offending Anglicisms; the Superior Council of the French Language mandates changes from Franglais to French substitutes; and the Francophone High Council, a body of French-speaking countries, promotes the international use of French (its secretary-general once suggested that it is better not to speak French at all than to speak it badly).

Although the 1992 edition of the Académie Française dictionary (the first revision since 1935) does admit some 6,000 new words to the French language, including, for the first time, a number of Franglais words and expressions, most of them are from the 1950s (*le cover girl, le bestseller, le blue-jeans*). There are very few if any computer or "pop" terms, words nonetheless in widespread use by French speakers. According to Maurice Druon, secretary of the Academy, the new dictionary includes Franglais words only "when there is not an honest French word for saying the same thing or expressing the same idea." "We are a kind of tribunal," he explained. "We baptize new words. It's not censoring; it's a confirmation of good usage. We give a sense of sin."

French linguistic chauvinism (if they didn't actually invent chauvinism, the French gave it a name, after Nicolas Chauvin, a fanatical Napoleonic soldier) has periodically reared its ugly *tête* since the Académie Française was formed in 1634 by Cardinal Richelieu to defend the purity of the French language. By that time French had long been a lingua franca, once so pervasive that the Italian Marco Polo used it to write his famous travelogue in 1298. By the end of the eighteenth century, all the courts of Europe were conducting their official business in French, and King Frederick the Great of Prussia was sponsoring a contest for the best French-language essay on "The Universality of the French Language." But as the British Empire expanded and the United States emerged as an economic and political force, so began the French decline that has accelerated since 1919, when the Treaty of Versailles was written in English as well as French.

French politicians have not taken this lying down. Their language police are trying to preserve the French of the glory days, when it was relatively free from foreign influences. In 1992 the French parliament passed an amendment to the French constitution that reads, "The language of the Republic is French." A group of French intellectuals applauded the amendment, denounced French "angloglots," and lamented the process of "linguistic debasement" and "collective self-destruction" resulting from the use of Franglais. And in 1994, the French Assembly passed an even tougher law requiring the use of the French language in everything from contracts to advertising billboards to instructions for appliances. (In a refreshing moment of lucidity, France's Constitutional Council ruled the law invalid on the ground that the government could legally police itself, but could not dictate language usage to individuals). The irony is, of course, that French is itself a combination of Latin, Arabic, Spanish, German, Greek, and, yes, English.

Theoretically, the validity of an official program to "purify" a language depends on one's point of view. It's either a gallant defense of standards in the face of linguistic barbarism, or intellectual totalitarianism. It's either a quixotic attempt to shield a language from "corruption," or a narrow-minded effort to keep it from being revitalized. Theoretically. In practice, it's just futile, because the value of a word depends on usage, not ideology. Language develops on its own, without regard to official policy. Such protectionist measures as constitutional amendments and fiat vocabularies are destined to fail because they run counter to the inexorable process of language hybridization.

Language hybridization (linguistic reactionaries would probably call it miscegenation resulting from promiscuous bilingualism) is a dynamic, relentless natural force, the inevitable result of a shrinking world. But it is nothing new; all the world's languages are products of cross-pollination. A large percentage of English originates in Latin and Greek, and many Asian languages share common roots.

Having lost its influence in many areas of human endeavor, official France has tried to salvage its image by attempting to preserve the French language in amber. At the same time English, grammatically simple, flexible, and pragmatic, has been structurally receptive to foreignisms. If there's a linguistic trade imbalance in favor of English, it is not because of any "predatory" practices. We Americans don't export our language, the French (and much of the rest of the world) import it, and no amount of linguistic protectionism will change that.

g

gabelle (gah **bel**) a tax on French salt first levied in 1286, and later under a system whereby all the salt produced in France was deposited in government warehouses and sold at artificially high prices. Some provinces received favorable prices at the expense of others, and everyone over the age of eight was required to purchase a minimum weekly quantity of salt. The *gabelle* was justly abolished in 1790, but the word is still occasionally applied to an indirect tariff.

gaffe (gahf) a blunder; a tactless comment.

gaga (gah **gah**) silly; crazy; wildly infatuated; doddering; senile.

gamine (gah **meen**) female street urchin; tomboy.

> If one looks upon fashion as the extension of warfare by other means, then the news that *gamines* are making a comeback is the sartorial equivalent of the Visigoths arriving at the outskirts of Rome. A *gamine*, for those young enough and lucky enough to have grown up in a *gamine*-less society, is defined by Webster as "a girl who likes to hang out in the streets" and also as "a small, playfully mischievous girl." A *gamine* is a cross between an urchin and a tomboy, with just a dash of the rapscallion and the scalawag thrown in for good measure.
>
> —JOE QUEENAN, *Washington Post*

gaminerie (gah **meen** ree) the sauciness of a street urchin.

garçon (gahr so^n) boy; waiter. From the Old French *garçun*, "servant."

garde du corps (**gahr** dü **kohr**) bodyguard.

gastronome (**gah** stroh nohm) a *connoisseur* (which see) of fine food and wine.

gâteau (gah **toh**) cake.

gauche (gohsh) "left hand"; tactless; vulgar; awkward. From the Old French *gauchir*, "to turn aside, shuffle; to walk clumsily."

(la) gauche ([lah] **gohsh**) (the) political left.

gauche caviar (**gohsh** kahv **yahr**) "caviar left"; the rough equivalent of "limousine liberal."

> Mitterrand offered a new aristocracy. In the early 1980s he gave up socialism—it turns out it doesn't work—and brought the country's mediagenic elite into his cabinet. They created a sybaritic personal style that became known as *gauche caviar.*
>
> —DAVID BROOKS, *National Review*

gaucherie (goh **shree**) clumsiness; vulgarity.

> Perhaps this salesperson knew just by glancing at me that I couldn't afford the wallet, even before I committed the terrible *gaucherie* of asking how much it cost.
>
> —DIANE WHITE, *Boston Globe*

genre (zha^n ruh) kind; sort; a type or style of art, literature, or film. From the Latin *genus*, a class or group with common attributes.

gens de bien (zha^n duh bye^n) respectable people.

gens d'église (zha^n day **gleez**) church people; clergy.

gens de guerre (zha^n duh **gehr**) military people.

gens du monde (zha^n dü mo^{n}d) "people of the world"; high society.

gigot (zhee **goh**) a leg of lamb; named for the *gigue*, an ancient musical instrument it is said to resemble.

glissade (glee **sahd**) a controlled slide, as on a slippery surface; a gliding ballet step.

(la) gloire ([lah] gluh **wahr**) (the) glory; honor.

> In a well-defined civilization with a solid historical background, such as for instance the French, you can easily discover the key-

note of the French *esprit*: it is *la gloire*, a most marked prestige psychology in its noblest as well as its most ridiculous forms. You find it in their speech, gestures, beliefs, in the style of everything, in politics, and even in science.

—C. G. JUNG, *The Complications of American Psychology*

gouache (gwash) a technique of applying opaque watercolor mixed with a preparation of gum to paper; a painting so produced.

gourmand (goor **mah**^{n}) a lover of good food, usually in large quantities; a glutton. Cf. *gourmet*.

gourmet (goor **may**) a person with a refined appreciation of superior food and wine. According to *Larousse Gastronomique*, there is a hierarchy of food lovers which "starts at the bottom with the *goinfre* (greedyguts), progresses to the *goulou* (glutton), then the *gourmand*, the *friand* (epicure), and the *gourmet*, and finally the *gastronome*."

grand amateur (grah^n dah mah **tuhr**) a great collector; one who loves beautiful objects.

grand coup (grah^n **koo**) a bold stroke; a great success.

grande amoureuse (grah^n **dah** moo **ruhz**) great (female) lover; a woman who devotes her life to love affairs.

(la) Grande Armée ([lah] grah^n dahr **may**) "(the) Great Army," a 500,000-man force assembled by Napoléon Bonaparte (1769–1821) for the invasion of Russia in 1812.

French is the language that turns dirt into romance.
—STEPHEN KING, *Time*, October 6, 1986

---

grande cocotte (grah^{n}d koh **koht**) an expensive prostitute; a kept woman.

At a time in France when young women were thought of as belonging to one of two types, either as *femmes honnêtes* or as *filles publiques*, women who hung around painters' studios tended to be consigned to the second category. (Its gradations from common prostitutes at the lower end of the scale to the *grandes cocottes* at the top may be studied in the fiction of Maupassant and Colette.)

—ANTHONY CURTIS, *Financial Times* (London)

grande dame (grah^{n}d **dahm**) great lady.

To board the Sea Cloud is to step into a gilded age. Private and pricey, this is a *grande dame* of the sea.

—SHERRI DALPHONSE, *Washingtonian*

grande passion (grah^{n}d pah syo^n) an all-consuming love; also, a passion fruit-and-Armagnac liqueur.

Invitation to the Married Life [by Angela Huth] . . . is a novel of middle age, focusing on four couples, a bachelor and his painter mother, and it involves *petits amours*, on the whole, rather than *grandes passions*.

—CHARLES A. BRADY, *Buffalo News*

Grand Guignol (grah^n **gee** nyohl) a series of eighteenth-century puppet plays involving violent and bloody incidents; the Parisian theater in which they were performed; anything gruesome or macabre.

Nothing could be farther from the *Grand Guignol* horrors of "Macbeth" than the courtly "Twelfth Night"—at least on the surface.

—SID SMITH, *Chicago Tribune*

grand luxe (grah^n **lüks**) "great luxury"; the highest class (of travel).

The incident involved Drexel Burnham Lambert and Michael Milken, and it marked the end of an era. Only it had nothing to do with junk bonds or hostile takeovers, as such. Instead, the firm's fall 1989 decree that the junk bond king's lawyer, Arthur Liman, could no longer bill first-class airfare to Drexel symbolically brought the front-of-the-fuselage curtain down on Wall Street's 1980s epic of *grand luxe* travel.

—LOIS MADISON REAMY, *Institutional Investor*

grand monde (grah^n mo^{n}d) "great world"; high society.

(le) grand peut-être ([luh] **grah**ⁿ puh **teht** ruh) "the great perhaps," the afterlife. The French physician and humanist François Rabelais (c. 1494–c. 1553) is credited with the deathbed declaration, *"Je m'en vais chercher un grand peut-être,"* "I go to seek the great perhaps."

Grand Prix (grahⁿ **pree**) "grand prize"; an international road race for Formula One cars; the *Grand Prix de Paris* at Longchamp, a famous horse race.

grand seigneur (grahⁿ seh **nyuhr**) a feudal lord; a great nobleman.

> Arafat and his men have all the time in the world. They live in villas, travel around in private planes, take part in congresses as representatives of a sovereign state, and play the *grand seigneur*.
>
> —TEDDY PREUSS, *Jerusalem Post*

(le) Grand Siècle ([luh] grahⁿ see **ehk** luh) the age of Louis XIV (1643–1715).

gratin (grah **ta**ⁿ) a topping of browned bread crumbs or cheese; a dish so prepared; the "upper crust" of society.

guardez la foi (gahr **day** lah **fwah**) keep the faith.

(la) guerre ([lah] gehr) war.

guerre à outrance (**gehr** ah oo **trah**ⁿs) war to the utmost; all-out war.

(la) guerre!—c'est une chose trop grave pour la confier à des militaires. ([lah] **gehr** say tuⁿ shohz **troh** grahv poor lah koⁿ **fyay** ah day mee lee **tehr**) "War is much too serious a matter to be entrusted to the military." The remark is attributed to both Charles-Maurice de Talleyrand-Périgord (1754–1838) and Georges Clemenceau (1841–1929). It is often translated as, "War is much too serious to leave to the generals."

guillotine (gee uh teen) A machine in which a large blade set between grooved posts falls upon and decapitates its victim. The "national razor" was the invention of Dr. Joseph-Ignace Guillotin (1738–1814), an anatomy professor who in 1789 recommended the device as the most humane method of executing members of the *ancien régime* (which see) and other enemies of the Revolution (who had previously been dispatched by various other means, including burning, hanging, and torture). The guillotine was first used on a forger named Pelletier on April 25, 1792, and nine months later to execute Louis XVI (1754–93). About three thousand victims were guillotined during the Reign of Terror.

Many nineteenth-century Americans on grand tours to Europe tried to take in at least one guillotining during their travels. . . . By 1853 the reductions of regional executioners in France led to the public auctioning of scaffolds and accessories in regions where they could no longer be of service. Often the wood was rotten and the metal rusty. Collectors began buying guillotines, and they began to show up at fairs as macabre attractions. Some executioners and their widows kept the machines, particularly the blades of supposedly "historic" guillotines, and later sold them to collectors at high prices. A number of blades "certified" to have decapitated Louis XVI were put up for sale over the years.

—DANIEL GEROULD, *Guillotine, Its Legend and Lore*

habitué (ah bee tü **ay**) regular customer; frequent visitor.

habitué de la maison (ah bee tü **ay** duh lah may **zo**ⁿ) a regular customer at a restaurant.

haute bourgeoisie (**oht** boor zhwah **zee**) upper–middle class.

haute couture (**oht** koo **tür**) high fashion.

haute cuisine (**oht** kwee **zeen**) the art of fine cooking.

haute époque (**oht** ay **pohk**) the period in France from 1643 to 1792, spanning the reigns of Louis XIV, XV, and XVI.

hauteur (oh **tuhr**) "height"; haughtiness; arrogance.

haut monde (oh **mo**ⁿd) high society.

> Marcel Deshabille is the most original and certainly the most controversial designer in pants, not to mention in France. His unique styles are the talk of the *haut monde* from Palm Springs to Rome and it is rumored that two editors of *W* became nudists after his last major show.
>
> —**LARRY TRITTEN,** *Seattle Times*

haute vulgarisation (**oht** vül gah ree zah **syo**ⁿ) "high popularization"; the art of making a difficult subject understandable to the masses.

hommage (oh **mahzh**) homage; respect; tribute.

> *Fallen Angels* is an *hommage* to forties Hollywood *film noir*, so it sounds like *faux* Hammett and Hemingway *manqué*, and is hard on women.
>
> —**JOHN LEONARD,** *New York*

homme d'affaires (**ohm** dah **fehr**) man of business; business agent.

homme de coeur (**ohm** duh **kuhr**) sensitive man. The classical usage was "man of courage."

homme d'esprit (**ohm** deh **spree**) man of wit; intellectual.

homme d'état (**ohm** day **tah**) statesman.

homme de lettres (**ohm** duh **leh** truh) man of letters.

homme du monde (**ohm** dü **mo^{n}d**) man of the world.

> Sir, Joe Rogaly, in his column 'Beurre Heseltine' (February 21), describes Mrs. Margaret Thatcher as "She who regarded herself as the *sole bonne femme.*" I cannot believe this to be true. *Une bonne femme* denotes a total lack of sophistication, namely a woman down at heel and rather vulgar. Mrs Thatcher may well have seen herself as the sole *grande dame* as she assumed the airs of an absolutist monarch. I suggest that he who regards himself as *un homme du monde* should first check his French.
>
> —HELENE SEPPAIN, letter to the *Financial Times* (London)

homme moyen sensuel (**ohm** mwah **ya^n** sah^n sü el) "man of moderate desires"; average man; man in the street.

> Rabbit has served Updike well in the past as the quintessential American *homme moyen sensuel* in *Run, Redux* and *Rich.*
>
> —JONATHAN RABAN, *Washington Post*

homme sensible (**ohm** sah^n see bluh) sensitive man.

homme sérieux (**ohm** say **ryuh**) serious man.

> Like him or not, Richard Nixon is what the French call an *homme sérieux,* a man of large vision who knows the world and whose views carry weight. However grudgingly, even those who hate his guts respect his mind. Even those who disagree most vehemently know that he thinks before he speaks.
>
> —RAYMOND K. PRICE, JR., *New York Times*

honnête homme (oh **net ohm**) an honest, respectable man; a gentleman.

hors commerce (**ohr** koh **mehrs**) "outside commerce"; not available through regular commercial channels.

hors concours (ohr ko^n **koor**) "outside the competition"; without equal.

hors de combat (ohr duh **kohm** bah) "outside the battle"; out of action; disabled; incapacitated.

"He levels his antagonists, he lays his friends low, and puts his own party *hors de combat*."

—WILLIAM HAZLITT of William Cobbett, *Table Talk, Essay VI*

hors-d'oeuvre (ohr **duh** vruh) "outside the work"; an appetizing tidbit served before a meal; a literary digression.

I can never remember how to spell *hors-d'oeuvre.* It shouldn't be that hard, but there is something about the combination of oeu that eludes my memory. *Hors-d'oeuvre* is a word or term that doesn't come up that often. Rarely do I have occasion to write it. And if a dictionary is not handy, I can always substitute *canapés.*

—JACK SMITH, *Los Angeles Times*

idée fixe (ee day **feeks**) "fixed idea"; fixation; obsession.

> Esperanto enjoyed a vogue for several generations. Only after two
> world wars did it subside into an *idée fixe* held by scattered fa-
> natics. Among them were my grandparents, who spoke it when
> they didn't want me to understand what they were talking about.
>
> —STEFAN KANFER, *The New Leader*

idée force (ee day **fors**) powerful idea.

idées reçues (ee day ruh sü) preconceived ideas; conventional
thinking.

il faut cultiver notre jardin (eel **foh** kül tee **vay** noh truh zhahr
da^n) "We must cultivate our garden." The final words, and
perhaps the moral, of Voltaire's *Candide*, suggesting that hu-
manity's proper sphere is self-improvement, not idle philo-
sophical speculation.

il n'est sauce que d'appétit (eel nay **sohs** kuh dah pay **tee**)
Hunger is the best sauce.

ils ne passeront pas (eel nuh pah sro^n **pah**) "They shall not
pass"; Marshal Pétain's (1856–1951) order at Verdun in Feb-
ruary 1916. They (the Germans) did not pass, and Pétain
became a national hero. Unfortunately, he lived long enough
to head the fascist Vichy régime, for which he was convicted
of treason in 1945.

immobiliste (ee **moh** bee **leest**) one opposed to progress or
reform; an ultraconservative; the opposite of a *progressiste*
(which see).

(les) Immortels ([lay] zee mohr **tel**) "the immortals"; the forty
members of the Académie Française (which see). The nickname is ostensibly derived from the slogan *"a l'immortalité"*

(les) Immortels

inscribed on the Academy's official seal, but since the members are elected for life, it may be a manifestation of Gallic irony.

ingénue (a^n zhay **nü**) an innocent young woman; the role of an innocent young woman in a theatrical production; an actress who plays such roles.

intime (a^n **teem**) intimate; cozy; confidential.

intrados (a^n **trah** doh) the inner curve of an arch or vault.

j'adoube (zhah **doob**) "I adjust"; in chess, a standard phrase when repositioning a piece without intending to move it.

j'accuse (zhah **küz**) "I accuse"; On January 13, 1898, the French newspaper *L'Aurore* published an open letter from the novelist Emile Zola (1840–1902) to the president of France denouncing the French army's treatment of Alfred Dreyfus (1859–1935), a Jewish officer who had been falsely convicted of espionage and imprisoned on Devil's Island. Through the efforts of Zola and other supporters, Dreyfus eventually received a new trial and a pardon. He was reinstated in the army and went on to serve with distinction during the First World War, retiring with the rank of lieutenant colonel. The closing paragraphs of Zola's celebrated polemic began with the words *j'accuse*, and the phrase has been associated with denunciation of bigotry and injustice ever since.

Jacobins (**zhah** koh ba[n]) a group of radical French intellectuals, including Marat, Danton, and Robespierre, whose revolutionary zeal sparked the Reign of Terror. The word comes from the Jacobin Club, named for the Dominican (*Jacobin*) convent where the group's meetings were held. *Jacobin* has since come to denote political extremism.

Jacquerie (zhah **kree**) a French peasant uprising against the nobility in 1358, and now any revolt of the peasantry (from *Jacques Bonhomme*, pejorative for a French peasant).

> With fighting talk on Saturday, Pierre Beregovoy, the Prime Minister, ruled out any prospect of abandoning France's vociferous peasantry. He was, in the words of one radio commentator . . . setting himself up as the leader of the *Jacquerie*, the fourteenth-

century peasant uprising evoked every time the farmers get restless.

—JULIAN NUNDY, *The Independent*

je ne sais quoi (zhuh nuh say **kwah**) I know not what; a certain indescribable something.

Je ne sais quoi is what you say in those awkward moments when you don't know what to say.

—HOWARD OGDEN, *Pensamentoes*

Je suis la France (zhuh **swee** lah **frah^{n}s**) "I am France"; Charles de Gaulle's oft-repeated claim during World War II (which reportedly never failed to infuriate Churchill).

jeté (zhuh **tay**) a ballet leap in which the dancer lands on one foot.

jeu de mots (zhuh duh **moh**) "game of words"; pun.

jeu d'esprit (zhuh deh **spree**) "game of the mind"; puzzle; witticism.

Another enemy of wit is American "pragmatism"—i.e., laziness. The pinnacle of wit is the *jeu d'esprit*—wit for its own sake, with no purpose but sheer joy in words. The *jeu d'esprit* should be popular in a country obsessed with games, but it collides with our preference for the quick 'n' easy. It takes a lot of reading and reflection to come up with puns, maxims, epigrams, and ripostes, but Americans can't be bothered.

—FLORENCE KING, *National Review*

jeu de théâtre (**zhuh** duh tay **ah** truh) stage trick; dramatic gesture.

jeune amour (**zhuhn** ah **moor**) young love.

jeune femme sérieuse (**zhuhn** fahm say **ryuhz**) an earnest young woman.

jeune refusé (**zhuhn** ruh fü **zay**) an angry young man.

jeune premier (**zhuhn** pruh **myay**) male juvenile lead (actor).

Nicholas Nickleby . . . is a brave and active, ingenuous *jeune premier* (very much in the Scott tradition) and cannot assume for us the qualities of a passive Blakean innocent like Oliver or Little Nell.

—MICHAEL SLATER, Introduction to *Nicholas Nickleby*
by Charles Dickens (Penguin Classics Edition)

jeunesse dorée (zhuh **ness** doh **ray**) "gilded youth"; affluent young people.

[During the] 72 hours of *Grand Prix* weekend, Monte Carlo stops looking like a James Bond film-set and starts behaving like one. In a stream of bright red Ferraris, the international jet set swarmed in, along the winding cliff roads from Nice and St. Tropez, while posses of *jeunesse dorée* were dropped from helicopters, private planes and a trail of boats that moored in the shadow of Stavros Niarchos's 4,500-ton yacht, Atlantis II.

—*Daily Telegraph* (London)

je vais rejoindre votre père (zhuh **vay** ruh **zhwa**^{n} druh **voh** truh **pehr**) "I go to rejoin your father"; Marie Antoinette's farewell to her children on being led to the guillotine.

joie de vivre (**zhwah** duh **vee** vruh) "joy of life"; zest for living; high spirits.

Over the years I have developed a distaste for the spectacle of *joie de vivre*, the knack of knowing how to live. Not that I disapprove of all hearty enjoyment of life. A flushed sense of happiness can overtake a person anywhere, and one is no more to blame for it than the Asiatic flu or a sudden benevolent change in the weather (which is often joy's immediate cause). No, what rankles me is the stylization of this private condition into a bullying social ritual.

—PHILLIP LOPATE, "Against Joie de Vivre"

jolie laide (zhoh **lee** led) a physically unattractive woman who somehow transcends her appearance to achieve a strange allure. Synonymous with *belle laide*.

journal intime (zhoor **nahl** a^n **teem**) "intimate journal"; confidential diary.

julienne (zhü **lyen**) to cut (especially vegetables) into thin strips.

juste milieu (zhüst mee **lyuh**) "golden mean"; balance; moderation.

j'y suis, j'y reste (zhee **swee**, zhee **rest**) "Here I am, here I remain"; the immortal declaration of French general Marie-Edmé MacMahon (1808–93) upon taking Sebastopol during the Crimean War.

k

képi (**kay** pee) a French military cap with a flat, circular top and a horizontal visor.

1

laissez-aller (**lay** say ah **lay**) "letting go"; lack of restraint.

laissez-faire (**lay** say **fehr**) "allow to do"; the doctrine of governmental noninterference, and by analogy any permissive attitude.

> Many were the black sheep of their respective families and were encouraged to go to California by relatives who were eager to have them transplanted several thousand miles from home. This accounts, Santa Barbarans say, for the special *laissez-faire* of the place—less grand and pretentious than Newport, less formal and competitive than Palm Beach.
>
> —STEPHEN BIRMINGHAM, *California Rich*

laissez-passer (**lay** say pah **say**) "allow to pass"; a diplomatic passport.

lamé (lah **may**) a metallic fabric made of interwoven threads.

l'argent (lahr **zhah**^{n}) money.

largesse (lahr **zhess**) bounty; generosity.

> In what some may see as another dose of election-year *largesse*, President Bush today announced he will recommend a multi-billion-dollar sale of U.S. jet fighters to Saudi Arabia.
>
> —BERNARD SHAW, CNN

Larousse Gastronomique (lah **roos** gah stroh noh **meek**) An encyclopedia of classical French cooking first published in 1938 and known worldwide as the "chef's Bible." With such entries as "Carving a *gigot* using meat-carving tongs," "hare mousse," and 295 different ways to prepare eggs not including omelettes, *Larousse Gastronomique* is widely regarded as the definitive reference for professional cooks. The lavishly illustrated, 1,200-page *New American Edition*, published in

1988 and edited by Jenifer Harvey Lang, bills itself as "the world's greatest culinary encyclopedia," and it lives up to the claim, though some of the translated-from-the-French entries are quaint and quirky, e.g., "Watermelon: A large spherical or oval fruit . . . with a dark green skin and pink flesh that is sweet and very refreshing but slightly insipid."

légèreté (lay zhehr **tay**) "lightness"; levity; frivolity.

Légion d'Honneur (lay **zhyo**ⁿ doh **nuhr**) "Legion of Honor"; a French government award in recognition of military or civilian merit instituted by Napoléon I in 1802. There are five classes: *Chevalier, Officier, Commandeur, Grand-Officier,* and *Grand-Croix.*

Légion étrangère (lay **zhyo**ⁿ nay trah**ⁿ zhehr**) Foreign Legion, an elite, all-volunteer unit of the French army composed of non-French troops. Founded in 1831 to help conquer Algeria, the French Foreign Legion has an aura of mystery and romance, in part due to its policy of giving enlistees a new identity. It is thus known as a refuge where a man of action can go to "forget and be forgotten."

légume (lay **güm**) vegetable.

lèse-majesté (**layz** mah zhay **stay**) "injured majesty"; an affront to the sovereign; high treason.

> Eventually, I came to understand that [Irving "Swifty"] Lazar simply refuses to believe that people close to him can be upset, or miserable, or unpleasant. Like the Sun King, he believes that his presence makes people happy, and therefore takes unhappiness as a kind of *lèse-majesté*.
>
> —MICHAEL KORDA, *The New Yorker*

German is of stone, limestone, pudding stone, marble, granite even, and so to a considerable degree is English, whereas French is bronze and gives out a metallic resonance with tones that neither German nor English tolerate.
—BERNARD BERENSON

l'état c'est moi (lay **tah** say **mwah**) "I am the state"; attributed to Louis XIV (1638–1715).

lettre de cachet (**leh** truh duh kah **shay**) a letter from the king of France ordering the governor of the Bastille to imprison a named person; any unjust arrest warrant.

liaison (lyay **zo**^{n}) a link or connection between groups; a go-between; illicit sexual relations.

liberté, égalité, fraternité (lee behr **tay**, ay gah lee **tay**, frah tehr nee **tay**) "liberty, equality, brotherhood"; a slogan of the French Revolution.

lingerie (la^n **zhree**) women's underwear. From *linge*, "linen." A prime example of a Frenglish word—pronounced (lai^n zhe **ray**) by Americans—that would be unrecognizable to the French, who pronounce it with two syllables, the middle *e* sound being virtually inaudible.

littérateur (**lee** tay rah **tuhr**) man of letters; literary critic.

livre de chevet (**lee** vruh duh shuh **vay**) "bedside book"; a favorite book.

livre rouge (**lee** vruh **roozh**) "red register"; Louis XVI's personal account book, which, made public by the National Assembly in April 1790, revealed his criminal extravagance.

loi de guerre (**lwah** duh **gehr**) rules of war.

longueur (lo^n **guhr**) "length"; a tedious passage in a work of music or literature.

> Listening to the *longueurs* of Wagner, he wishes he could hit a fast-forward button.
>
> —MATTHEW GUREWITSCH, *The Atlantic*

lorgnette (lohr **nyet**) a pair of eyeglasses with a long handle; opera glasses.

l'oubli (**loo** blee) "the forgetfulness"; the tendency of the French public to ignore the Vichy regime's collaboration with the Nazis during World War II.

louche (loosh) shady; disreputable.

> I know of a *louche* little bar quite near here.
>
> —EVELYN WAUGH, *Brideshead Revisited*

Louis Quatorze (loo ee kah **tohrz**) King Louis XIV (1638–1715). Called *le Grand Monarque* and *le Roi Soleil* (the Sun King), he was a prodigious figure whose reign, from 1643 to 1715, was the longest in European history. An absolute monarch perhaps best remembered for the remark, *l'état c'est moi* (which see), his reign coincided with a golden age of French arts and letters, but his extravagances helped bankrupt his country.

Louis Quinze (loo ee ka^{n}z) King Louis XV of France (1710–74), nicknamed *le Bien-Aimé* (the Beloved). His sixty-year reign (from 1715 to 1774) was marked by social strife, economic instability, and a series of French defeats abroad, including the loss of territories during the Seven Years' War (1756–63).

Louis Seize (loo ee sez) King Louis XVI of France (1754–93), who reigned from 1774 to 1792 with his wife, Marie Antoinette. Both his reign and his life were ended violently by the French Revolution.

Louis Treize (loo ee trez) King Louis XIII of France (1601–43), nicknamed *le Juste* (the Just) who reigned from 1610 to 1643.

m

madeleine (mahd **len**) a rich, oval-shaped French cookie. In Proust's *À la recherche du temps perdu* (which see) the act of dipping a *madeleine* in a cup of tea transports the author back to his childhood. The word has thus come to denote an object or sensation that triggers deep memories.

> The Proust *madeleine* phenomenon is now as firmly established in folklore as Newton's apple or Watt's steam kettle. The man ate a tea biscuit, the taste evoked memories, he wrote a book. This is capable of expression by the formula TMB, for Taste > Memory > Book. Some time ago, when I began to read a book called *The Food of France*, by Waverly Root, I had an inverse experience: BMT, for Book > Memory > Taste. Happily, the tastes that *The Food of France* re-created for me—small birds, stewed rabbit, stuffed tripe, Côte Rôtie, and Tavel—were more robust than that of the *madeleine*, which Larousse defines as a "light cake made with sugar, flour, lemon juice, brandy, and eggs." (The quantity of brandy in a *madeleine* would not furnish a gnat with an alcohol rub.) In the light of what Proust wrote with so mild a stimulus, it is the world's loss that he did not have a heartier appetite. On a dozen Gardiners Island oysters, a bowl of clam chowder, a peck of steamers, some bay scallops, three sautéed soft-shelled crabs, a few ears of fresh-picked corn, a thin swordfish steak of generous area, a pair of lobsters, and a Long Island duck, he might have written a masterpiece.
>
> —A. J. LIEBLING, "A Good Appetite"

ma foi (mah **fwah**) "My faith!"; indeed!

maillot jaune (mah **yoh** zhohn) the traditional yellow jersey awarded to the daily leader of the Tour de France (which see).

maison close (may **zo**^{n} klohz) brothel.

maison de rendezvous (may zoⁿ duh rahⁿ day **voo**) an inn or hotel specializing in accommodating lovers' *rendezvous* (which see).

maison de santé (may zoⁿ duh sahⁿ **tay**) sanitarium; private hospital.

maison de société (may zoⁿ duh soh syay **tay**) brothel.

maison tolérée (may zoⁿ toh lay **ray**) a brothel licensed and inspected by the state.

maître de cuisine (**meh** truh duh kwee **zeen**) master cook; head chef.

maître d'hôtel (**meh** truh doh **tel**) head waiter; chief steward. What we Americans call a "maytra dee."

maîtresse en titre (**meh** tress ahⁿ **tee** truh) an "official" mistress; that is, a long-term mistress as opposed to a casual *liaison* (which see).

malade imaginaire (mah **lahd** ee mah zhee **nehr**) "imaginary invalid"; a hypochondriac (from Molière's "*Le Malade Imaginaire*" [1673]).

malaise (mah **lez**) a vague feeling of physical or mental discomfort.

> One year after the crash, the markets remain mired in a deep *malaise*.
>
> —*New York Times*

maladroit (mahl ah **drwah**) clumsy; awkward; inept.

mal à propos (**mahl** ah proh **poh**) "out of place"; inappropriate; unsuitable. This expression, a first cousin to the English words malaprop and malapropism, is the etymological basis for "Mrs. Malaprop," a character in Richard Brinsley Sheridan's play *The Rivals* (1775) who liked to use big words but often confused them, that is, she used them *mal à propos*. Thus she advised a young woman to "illiterate" a certain gentleman from her memory, described someone as "the very pineapple of politeness," and said of herself: "If I reprehend anything in this world, it is the use of my oracular tongue, and a nice derangement of epitaphs!"

mal de mer (**mahl** duh **mehr**) "evil of the sea"; seasickness.

mal du pays (**mahl** dü pay ee) homesickness.

mal du siècle (**mahl** dü see **ay** kluh) world-weariness; weltschmerz.

> Two brothers, Frederick and Charles Courtland, [are] seeking their fortunes in the glittering metropolis. One is an architect, fascinated by the new technology of ironwork; the other is a spoiled priest, inspired by the new creed of skepticism. Both are struggling hard with the *mal du siècle*, the Romantic disease of the imagination, that makes it so difficult to convert private dreams into sustained social realities.
>
> —RICHARD HOLMES, *New York Times*

malentendu (**mahl** ah[n] tah[n] dü) misunderstanding; misapprehension.

> An extraordinary *malentendu* appears to have been at the root of recent riots in Guinea, West Africa. When Alseny Gomez, a Spanish businessman, was reported to have offered young women money to be filmed having sex with dogs, angry mobs tried to lynch him and then ran amok for three days in Conakry, the capital, stoning foreigners' cars and raping Guinean women dressed in Western-style clothes. But last week, after dogged investigations, the interior minister said the Spaniard's nightwatchman had made up the stories to scare off a girlfriend who was demanding money.
>
> —*Times* (London)

malgré lui (**mahl** gray **lwee**) in spite of himself/herself; against his/her will or better judgment. In *Le Médecin malgré lui*, a comedy by Molière, a woodcutter named Sganarelle poses as a doctor against his better judgment.

malgré moi (**mahl** gray **mwah**) in spite of myself; against my will.

malgré tout (**mahl** gray **too**) in spite of everything.

mal mariée (**mahl** mah ree **yay**) an unhappily married woman.

mal soigné (**mahl** swahn **yay**) unkempt; shabby.

mal vu (mahl **vü**) badly regarded; resented; disapproved of.

manqué (mah^n **kay**) failed; frustrated; unsuccessful in fulfilling one's goals or aspirations. The past participle of the verb *manquer*, "to spoil, make a mess of."

> She [Tina Brown] said it has taken a long time to get The Talk of the Town section to hit its stride, but thinks it has now. "It had become too much of a *belles-lettres* wannabe and E. B. White *manqué*," she said, referring to the great *New Yorker* writer. "My feeling is if you don't have E. B. White, then don't have E. B. White *manqué*."
>
> —DEIRDRE CARMODY, *New York Times*

manque de goût (mah^{n}k duh **goo**) absence of good taste.

maquis (mah **kee**) French guerrilla fighters during World War II, better known as la Résistance. *Maquis* is actually Corsican for the thick, impenetrable underbrush which served as a hideout for Corsican bandits. The World War II use was thus meant to imply a kind of "underground opposition."

maréchal (may ray **shahl**) field marshal.

mariage de convenance (mah **ryahzh** duh **ko**^{n} vuh **nah**^{n}s) marriage of convenience.

> The IBM/Apple *mariage de convenance* can be explained in terms of social set theory wherein partitions of less-threatening partners arise among mutually hostile members. If A and B hate C more than they hate each other . . . the details are left as an exercise for the reader.
>
> —STAN KELLY-BOOTLE, *Unix Review*

mari complaisant (mah **ree** kohm play **sah**^{n}) "complacent husband"; a man who tolerates his wife's infidelity.

marmot (mahr **moh**) "little monkey"; a small, freakish person.

(la) Marseillaise ([lah] **mahr** say **yez**) the French national anthem, written by French army engineer Rouget de Lisle on April 25, 1792, upon the French declaration of war on Austria. Its original title, *Chant de guerre pour l'armée du Rhin*

("Song of the Rhine Army"), was changed to *la Marseillaise* after it was sung by a band of Marseilles volunteers, first as they marched to Paris, and later during the storming of the Tuileries Palace on August 10, 1792. Ironically, Rouget de Lisle was a royalist who refused to take the oath of allegiance to the revolutionary government, and he was imprisoned and barely escaped execution.

The melody is familiar to Americans, partly from the "dueling anthems" scene in *Casablanca* (1942) in which the refugees at Rick's *Café Americaine* spontaneously break into the *Marseillaise* in order to drown out the German anthem sung by Nazi officers.

Of the original six stanzas (a seventh, known as the "Children's stanza," was added later), the first and sixth are best known. The words *"Allons, enfants de la patrie"* refer literally to a battalion of teenage boys who volunteered to fight the Austrian and Prussian invaders:

> *Allons, enfants de la patrie!*
> *Le jour de gloire est arrivé!*
> *Aux armes! citoyens, Formez vos bataillons!*
> *Marchons! marchons! qu'un sang impur*
> *Abreuve nos sillons!*
>
> Forward, sons of France,
> the day of glory has come!
> To arms, citizens! Line up in battalions!
> Let us march on! And let the impure blood [of our enemies]
> drench our fields.

Nothing like the *Marseillaise* has ever been written that comes so near to expressing the comradeship of citizens in arms and nothing ever will.

—SIMON SCHAMA, *Citizens*

martinet (mahr tee **nay**) a spit-and-polish military man; a strict disciplinarian. The Marquis de Martinet, a French officer and the commander of Louis XIV's personal regiment, instituted a rigorous system of drilling and generally maintained harsh discipline in the ranks of the French infantry, which he also commanded. Perhaps not coincidentally, he was killed by "friendly" artillery fire while leading an assault at the siege of Duisburg in 1672.

masque (mahsk) "mask"; an allegorical dramatic form which originated in the courts of Europe during the sixteenth century.

matériel (mah tay **ryel**) military supplies and equipment.

matinée musicale (mah tee **nay** mü zee **kahl**) a concert given in the afternoon.

> Authenticity . . . impelled Mr. Schlondorff to cast French aristocrats in the role of French aristocrats. The call sheet for the *matinée musicale* at the Guermantes's contain some of France's noblest titles. Counts, dukes, and princes jumped at the chance to rub shoulders with movie stars. "Of course I cast aristocrats as extras," Mr. Schlondorff confesses. "I didn't have to pay them, and in Proust it's important to have the right wallpaper. Besides, they were very well-behaved—exquisite manners. After the last day of shooting one of them tiptoed up to me and whispered, 'How much of a gratuity should one leave for the makeup man?' "
>
> —ARTHUR HOLMBERG, *New York Times*

mauvais goût (**moh** vay **goo**) bad taste.

> In the nation's capital, where knowledge is power, giving out information—or, more important, withholding it—has been developed to a high art. . . . "No comment" reeks of the hinterlands. "Drop dead" is at best *mauvais goût*. And feigning laryngitis arouses suspicions.
>
> —WAYNE KING, *New York Times*

mauvais quart d'heure (**moh** vay kahr **duhr**) "bad quarter-hour"; a brief but uncomfortable experience.

> By helping Jerry [Langford] out of the mauling clutches of rabid fans one night, then insinuating himself into the star's limousine, Rupert starts what he takes for a professional and personal relationship, and Langford for a mere *mauvais quart d'heure*.
>
> —JOHN SIMON, *National Review*

méchant (may **shah**^{n}) naughty; malicious.

mélange (may **lahnzh**) medley; mixture; conglomeration.

mêlée (meh **lay**) hand-to-hand combat; a brawl or free-for-all; a scuffle or crush. From the Old French *mesler*, "to mix."

mémoire (maym **wahr**) "memory"; written recollections; autobiographical narrative.

mémoire involontaire (maym **wahr** a^n voh lo^n **tehr**) a sudden memory triggered by a smell, a taste, or a physical sensation (from Proust's *A la recherche du temps perdu*).

> He opened the door, and I slipped into the passenger's seat. I was instantly seized with a sensation that I couldn't have been prepared for, that sudden excitement you feel when you stumble upon some childhood experience long since forgotten, an awakening of memory stirred by the odor of gym shoes or burning leaves—what Proust described as *mémoire involontaire*.
>
> —JAMES ATLAS, *New York Times*

ménage (may **nahzh**) household; housekeeping; a couple living together.

ménage à trois (may **nahzh** ah **trwah**) specifically, a household of three consisting of a couple plus either his mistress or her lover; generally, a threesome; also, a sexual encounter involving three people.

mésalliance (may zah **lyah^{n}s**) an unsuitable marriage; a mismatch; marriage beneath oneself.

> The London securities market may be flinging itself into a *mêlée* of alliances and *mésalliances* in preparation for the Big Bang, but to the money market so many of the "innovations" that deregulation will introduce are distinctly *passé*.
>
> —ALICE RAWSTHORN, *Financial Times* (London)

métier (may **tyay**) an occupation, trade, or specialty; an area of activity to which one is especially suited.

> For me, writing is the only thing that passes the three tests of *métier*: (1) when I'm doing it, I don't feel I should be doing some-

thing else instead; (2) it produces a sense of accomplishment and, once in a while, pride; and (3) it's frightening.

—GLORIA STEINEM

Métro (may **troh**) the Parisian subway system, shorthand for *chemin de fer Métropolitain.*

milieu (meel **yuh**) setting; atmosphere; social environment; intellectual climate.

minute de vérité (mee **nüt** duh vay ree **tay**) moment of truth; synonymous with *moment de vérité.*

mise en page (mee zah^n **pahzh**) layout; graphic design.

mise en scène (mee zah^n **sen**) stage setting; backdrop; surroundings.

> While banks of roses perfumed the air at one end of Paris, puddles of blood contaminated it at the other end. The guillotine had no place in the visual *mise en scène* of the Supreme Being, so Robespierre banished it from the place de la Révolution to the open space at the end of the rue Saint-Antoine that would become the Place de la Bastille.
>
> —SIMON SCHAMA, *Citizens*

mistral (mee **strahl**) a dry, cold, northwest wind that blows through the Rhône Valley toward the Mediterranean coast of southern France.

The country around Arles is the most torn, desperately lashed section in Provence. You've been out in that sun. Can't you imagine what it must do to these people who are subject to its blinding light day after day? I tell you, it burns the brains right out of their heads. And the *mistral.* You haven't felt the *mistral* yet? Oh, dear, wait until you do. It whips this town into a frenzy two hundred days out of every year. If you try to walk the streets, it smashes you against the buildings. If you are out in the fields, it knocks you down and grinds you into the dirt. It twists your insides until you think you can't bear it another minute. I've seen that infernal wind tear out windows, pull up trees, knock down fences, lash the men and animals in the fields until I thought they would surely fly in pieces. I've been here only three months, and I'm going a little *fou* myself.

—IRVING STONE, *Lust for Life*

mode nouvelle (**mohd** noo **vel**) "new style"; the latest fashion.

moeurs (**muhrs**) mores; attitudes; manners.

Disciplined Americans also manage queueing better. They separate skiers into queues and place queue-marshalls at strategic points so that every departing seat is filled. Europe seems incapable of such discipline. So many nations of clashing *moeurs* ski together that old rivalries explode into war in the ski queues.

—*The Economist*

moeurs de province (**muhrs** duh proh va^{n}s) local customs. *Moeurs de Province* is the subtitle Flaubert gave to *Madame Bovary*.

moment critique (moh **mah**^{n} kree **teek**) critical moment.

moment de vérité (moh **mah**^{n} duh vay ree **tay**) moment of truth. Synonymous with *minute de vérité*.

monde (**mo**^{n}d) "world"; society.

monologue intérieur (moh noh **lohg** a^n tay **ryuhr**) "interior monologue"; "stream of consciousness," a literary technique that portrays the thoughts and feelings in the mind of a fictional character directly, without the intervention of a narrator. Molly Bloom's musings in the final chapter of James Joyce's *Ulysses* are a prime example of the technique, but Joyce did not invent it: he acknowledged *Les Lauriers sont coupés* ("The Laurels Have Been Cut") (1888) by Edouard Dujardin as an antecedent.

monstre sacré (**mo**^{n} struh sah **kray**) "sacred monster"; a performer whose celebrity is enhanced by his or her eccentricities.

Rudolph Nureyev was more than a star; he was a *monstre sacré*, one of the few examples of the breed to arrive on the world's stage after the middle of the twentieth century.

—ARLENE CROCE, *The New Yorker*

monstre sacré

montage (moⁿ **tahzh**) a technique in which disparate visual elements are juxtaposed.

montagnard (moⁿ tahn **yahr**) "mountaineer"; a tribe inhabiting the highlands of Vietnam.

moral(e) (moh **rahl**) the spirit and cohesiveness of a group, especially a military unit.

morgue (mohrg) arrogance; haughtiness.

(la) morgue anglaise ([lah] mohrg ahⁿ **glez**) the haughtiness imputed to the English by the French.

> Dickens . . . evidently in the course of his astonishing rise, found himself up against the blank and chilling loftiness—what the French call *la morgue anglaise*—of the English upper classes.
>
> —EDMUND WILSON, "Dickens: The Two Scrooges"

mot à mot (moh ah moh) word for word; literally.

(le) mot juste ([luh] moh **zhoost**) the right word.

Flaubert's famous search for the ***mot juste*** was once described as the cork which, once pulled, opens the bottle. If I can get at the cork, I can get all the drops, too.

—VIKRAM SETH, *Vanity Fair*

musée imaginaire (mü **zay** ee mah zhee **nehr**) "imaginary museum"; a term coined by André Malraux in 1950 to describe the "museum of the mind" made possible by the existence of high-quality fine art reproductions.

n

naturel (nah tü **rel**) natural.

nature morte (nah **tür mohrt**) "dead nature"; a still life.

(le) néant ([luh] nay **ah**ⁿ) "non-being"; nothingness; emptiness.

(le) néant de la vie ([luh] nay **ah**ⁿ duh lah **vee**) the worthlessness of life.

> If only this damned French language were not so badly fitted for music!
> —WOLFGANG AMADEUS MOZART, *letter to his father*, July 9, 1778

---

née (nay) "born"; indicating a woman's maiden name.

n'est-ce pas? (nes **pah?**) Isn't it so?

niche (neesh) a recess in a wall for displaying statuary; a crevice or hollow in a rock; a field of endeavor to which a person is especially suited by skill or nature; an area of market demand for a product or service.

n'importe (**nam** pohrt) it's of no import; it doesn't matter.

noblesse oblige (noh **bless** oh **bleezh**) "nobility obliges"; people of privilege and high social rank are obligated to those less fortunate.

nocturne (**nohk** türn) "of night"; a painting of a night scene; a romantic, dreamy musical composition, usually for piano.

nom de guerre (nohm duh **gehr**) "war name"; pseudonym; professional name. The term may date to the Middle Ages, when it was customary for French army recruits to assume a new name, or it may derive from the medieval knights' practice of displaying, and being known by, the heraldic insignia on their shields.

nom de lieu (nohm duh **lyuh**) place name.

nom de plume (nohm duh **plüm**) "pen name"; a writer's pseudonym.

nom de théâtre (**nohm** duh tay **ah** truh) stage name; pseudonym.

nonpareil (no^n pah **ray**) matchless, unparalleled; without equal. Also, a small chocolate drop covered with white sugar pellets.

> VIOLA: I see you what you are, you are too proud;
> But, if you were the devil, you are fair.
> My lord and master loves you: O! such love
> Could be but recompensed, though you were crown'd
> The *nonpareil* of beauty.
>
> —WILLIAM SHAKESPEARE, *Twelfth Night or What You Will*,
> Act I, Scene 5

nostalgie de la boue (noh stahl **zhee** duh lah **boo**) "homesickness for the mud"; a longing for the low life; a craving for degradation.

> Radical chic, after all, is only radical in style; in its heart it is part of society and its traditions. Politics, like Rock, Pop, and Camp, has its uses; but to put one's whole status on the line for *nostalgie de la boue* in any of its forms would be unprincipled.
>
> —TOM WOLFE, *Radical Chic and Mau-Mauing the Flak Catchers*

nouveau riche (**noo** voh **reesh**) "new rich"; a derogatory term for those with newly acquired wealth. Cf. *arriviste, Bourgeois Gentilhomme, parvenu.*

nouveau roman (**noo** voh roh **mah**^{n}) "new novel"; a term coined in 1963 by Alain Robbe-Grillet to describe the experimental novels of such modern French writers as Marguerite Duras and Nathalie Sarraute.

nostalgie de la boue

In the field of art, as usual, the French have been propounding theory and expecting practice to follow, rather than—which is what Anglo-America prefers to do—theorizing out of art put together out of instinct. Thus, there has been the doctrine of the *nouveau roman*, or anti-novel, which, apart from the odd book by Robbe-Grillet and Nathalie Sarraute, has been more exciting to argue about than to see incarnated in an actual work of art.

—ANTHONY BURGESS, "Morbus Gallicus"

nouvelle (noo **vel**) "new"; a short novel; a novella.

nouvelle cuisine (noo **vel** kwee **zeen**) a revolutionary style of French cooking developed in the early 1970s, designed to replace rich, elaborate, and formalistic classic cuisine with healthier, more natural ingredients and aesthetic presentation. It favors fresh, crisp vegetables, light sauces, and rapid cooking with a minimum of fat and sugar. *Nouvelle cuisine* was something of a *cause célèbre* (which see): Its proponents proclaimed triumph over the "bourgeois cookery" of the nineteenth century, but its critics derided it as trendy and pretentious.

> The first course arrived. Fallow had ordered a vegetable *pâté*. The *pâté* was a small pinkish semicircle with stalks of rhubarb arranged around it like rays. It was perched in the upper left-hand quadrant of a large plate. The plate seemed to be glazed with an odd *Art Nouveau* painting of a Spanish galleon on a reddish sea sailing toward the . . . sunset . . . but the setting sun was, in fact, the *pâté*, with its rhubarb rays, and the Spanish ship was not done in glaze at all but in different colors of sauce. Ruskin's plate contained a bed of flat green noodles carefully intertwined to create a basket weave, superimposed upon which was a flock of butterflies fashioned from pairs of mushroom slices, for the wings; pimientos, onion slices, shallots, and capers, for the bodies, eyes, and antennae.

—TOM WOLFE, *The Bonfire of the Vanities*

Nouvelle Vague (noo vehl **vahg**) "New Wave"; a French cinematic style of the late 1950s and early 1960s that rejected "papa's cinema," the slick professionalism of Hollywood productions, in favor of a more personal style. Louis Malle, Alain Resnais, Claude Chabrol, Jean-Luc Godard, and François Truffaut were prominent New Wave directors. Leading examples of the short-lived genre are Godard's *Breathless* (1959), Truffaut's *Shoot the Piano Player* (1960), and Resnais's *Last Year at Marienbad* (1961).

nuance (nü ah^{n}s) a subtle difference in meaning or tone; a shade or gradation.

nuit blanche (nwee **blah^{n}sh**) "white night"; a sleepless night.

Down with Englench!

~

If they are declaring war on Franglais, I say that it is time for us to declare war on Englench. No matter what Jack Lang, French minister of culture, thinks, it is not the Americans who are cultural imperialists, or even imperialistes. It's the French. Who, after all, made us wear lingerie when our underwear was perfectly decent? Who turned our cooks into chefs and our dances into ballets? Where was it writ that a bunch of flowers had to become a bouquet? Or that toilet water had to be cologne, let alone perfume. What was the raison d'être for turning a decent American tenderloin into a chateaubriand?

What the French resent is not our imperialism but our democracy. We gave them McDonald's. They gave us the croissant. We gave them the ice-cream cone. They gave us quiche.

The people who invented the very word élite simply have a gripe against mass culture. They cheerfully export the notion that the only proper clothing is their couture and the only proper hairdo is their coiffure and the only proper food is their cuisine. Then they complain about "le jeans."

Through their own largesse, not to say noblesse oblige, they prefer to determine what is haute and what is not. They want the exclusive worldwide franchise to separate the chic from the gauche. If they want to ban Franglais, we will meet them at the beaches with boatloads of their own Englench. If they turn their drive-ins into cine-parcs, we shall turn our quiche into cheese pie. If they no longer attend le meeting we will no longer rendezvous.

If they make it de rigueur to eliminate Americanisms, we shall refuse to eat our apple pie à la mode and our soup du jour. We shall, in fact, hoist them on their own petulant petard.

And if the French decide to give up and return to the old laissez-faire linguistics, well, they better not call it détente.

ELLEN GOODMAN

O

objet d'art (ohb **zhay dahr**) art object; work of art.

objet de vertu (ohb **zhay** duh vehr **tü**) a work of art.

> Can the monarchy survive for long? When the Princess of Wales lends her illustrious name to the ragbag of Scottish disciplinarians, evangelical health fetishists, idle doctors and fresh air freaks gathered under the anti-smoking banner, we can say that her behaviour is just about within the acceptable limits of Royal eccentricity. One would prefer it, of course, if she took an interest in collecting ***objets de vertu*** from the homes of her friends, like dear old Queen Mary, but everybody needs a hobby.
>
> —ANONYMOUS, *Daily Telegraph*

objet trouvé (ohb **zhay** troo **vay**) "found object"; a natural object that acquires artistic value upon discovery by the finder.

> They were passionate about ***objets trouvés***. André Breton, the father of the [Surrealist] movement, was always snooping about in flea markets looking for strange and wonderful things wrenched out of context. It was he who said "Beauty will be convulsive, or not at all."
>
> —ELSPETH THOMPSON, *Daily Telegraph*

oeillade (wee **yahd**) a "meaningful" glance; a "come-hither" look.

oeuvre (**uh** vruh) "work"; a work of art or literature; the total body of work of an artist or writer.

> What on earth has made America's young audiences, who now know more about Wayne's World than John Wayne, go in such convincing numbers to see an elegiac Western that occupies roughly the same place in Eastwood's ***oeuvre*** as *Rio Bravo* did in that of Howard Hawks?
>
> —DEREK MALCOLM, *Manchester Guardian Weekly*

opéra bouffe (oh pay rah boof) light or comic opera (synonymous with *opéra comique*).

opéra comique (oh pay rah koh meek) light or comic opera (synonymous with *opéra bouffe*).

où sont les neiges d'antan? (oo so^n lay nehzh dah^n tah^n) "Where are the snows of yesteryear?" The refrain from *Ballade des dames du temps jadis* by François Villon (1431–?).

outré (oo tray) outrageous; bizarre; over the top.

> The *outré* quality of cigar smoking today also gives it a certain attraction. It is not merely a pleasure or an expensive pleasure but a defiant pleasure, and perhaps all the richer for it.
>
> —WILLIAM F. POWERS, *Washington Post*

p

Palme d'Or (pahlm **dohr**) "Golden Palm"; the prestigious best-film prize given at the Cannes Film Festival. Past winners include *La Dolce Vita*, *M*A*S*H*, *Apocalypse Now*, *Barton Fink*, and *The Piano*. The French pronounce the *l* in *Palme*, but most American Cannes–goers do not.

Palmes Académiques (**pahlm** zah kah day **meek**) "Academic Palms"; a French award for scholarship.

papier mâché (pah **pyay** mah **shay**) "chewed paper"; a molding material made of shredded paper soaked in starch or paste and used to create three-dimensional objects; an object so produced.

panache (pah **nahsh**) courage; spirit. Literally, the plume of feathers on the crest of an officer's helmet; figuratively, the verve or dash of one who wears it.

> It is worth remembering that the man who brought down Mrs. Thatcher was, of course, Sir Geoffrey Howe-dull-can-you-get. He is long mocked for having all the sparkle and *panache* of Hush Puppies.
>
> —PETER FREEDMAN, *Manchester Guardian Weekly*

Pangloss (pah^n **glohs**) a foolish optimist. From "Doctor Pangloss," the pedantic tutor in Voltaire's *Candide* (1759), named for the two Greek words meaning "explains everything." An eternal optimist, Pangloss's constant refrain, *"Tout est pour le mieux dans le meilleur des mondes possibles,"* "All is for the best in the best of all possible worlds," was Voltaire's mocking reply to the philosophers Leibniz and von Wolff, who had posited the existence of a benign providence in control of the world.

par excellence (pahr eks ay **la^{n}s**) the best of all; incomparable.

par exemple (pahr ehg **zahm** pluh) for example.

par hasard (pahr ah **zahr**) by chance; accidentally.

> To me, the soaps are comforting because you don't have to sit there with your critical faculties on red alert. I got into *Eldorado par hasard*, because it comes on soon after *Neighbours*. I didn't like it at first, but I'm addicted now.
>
> —ANNA SCHER, *Times* (London)

pari mutuel (pahr ee mü tü **el**) mutual betting; a system whereby losers' bets are paid to winners after the deduction of a fixed percentage.

parti pris (pahr tee **pree**) "side taken"; a preconceived opinion; bias; prejudice.

parvenu (pahr vuh **nü**) upstart; social climber. Cf. *arriviste, nouveau riche.*

> Churchill describes asking his bodyguard (detective) as they strolled in the grounds of a country house, what he thought of *that* . . . a heated swimming pool. The detective pursed his lips judiciously. "Frankly, sir, it smacks of the *parvenoo*."
>
> —JOHN TRAIN, *Valsalva's Maneuver*

pas de deux (**pah** duh **duh**) "dance for two"; metaphorically, the jockeying for position between two opponents.

pas d'ennemi à gauche (pah dayn **mee** ah **gohsh**) "No enemy on the left," i.e., France has nothing to fear from the political left wing.

pas devant les domestiques (pah duh **vah**[n] lay doh mes **teek**) "Not in front of the servants," a warning used by English-speakers not to discuss a confidential matter in the presence of the servants, who presumably do not understand French. See also, *pas devant les enfants.*

pas devant les enfants (pah duh **vah**[n] lay zah[n] **fah**[n]) "Not in front of the children." See also, *pas devant les domestiques.*

pas du tout (**pah** dü **too**) not at all.

pas possible (**pah** poh **see** bluh) impossible; it can't be done.

Lots of things in Paris work on the *"pas possible"* principle, meaning "we don't do it this way here, so tough luck for you if you want it otherwise."

—PATRICIA WELLS, *New York Times*

pasquinade (pahs kee **nahd**) satire; lampoon. From Pasquino, a fifteenth-century Italian barber on whose statue satires and political squibs were posted.

passé (pah **say**) out of fashion; outmoded.

"Getting pierced through the nose is *passé*," sniffs the 28-year-old Akron native who calls himself Dave. "Lips is my statement —at least for now."

—ROBERTO SANTIAGO, *Cleveland Plain Dealer*

passe-partout (pahs pahr **too**) "pass everywhere"; a passkey or master key. Also, the name of Phileas Fogg's unflappable valet in Jules Verne's *Around the World in Eighty Days* (1873).

passionnant (pah syo^n **nah**^{n}) exciting; invigorating; stirring.

passionné (pah syo^n **nay**) fan; aficionado.

pastiche (pahs **teesh**) an open imitation of a particular style; a takeoff; a hodgepodge of different styles.

French jazz-rock violinist [Jean-Luc] Ponty recorded this collection of Frank Zappa compositions with Zappa's band, the Mothers of Invention, with the maestro himself providing the arrangements and a taste of guitar, in the early '70s. The CD reissue offers a second look at a neglected gem, a brilliant instrumental *pastiche* that veers from dense, furious attacks to feather-light melodic flights.

—JOEL SELVIN, *San Francisco Chronicle*

pathétique (pah tay **teek**) "pathetic"; moving; touching; a musical term signifying deep feeling, which sometimes appears in the title of a work, such as Tchaikovsky's *Symphonie Pathétique* or Beethoven's *Pathétique Sonata*.

pâtisserie (pah tees **ree**) pastry; a pastry shop.

patois (pah **twah**) local or regional dialect; jargon; lingo.

pavé (pah **vay**) cobbled pavement; a technique whereby precious stones are set in a tight cluster resembling cobblestones.

paysage (pay ee **zahzh**) countryside; landscape; landscape painting.

peignoir (pen **wahr**) a woman's dressing gown originally designed to be worn while combing the hair (from *peigner*, "to comb").

pelisse (puh **lees**) a woman's fur-trimmed cloak.

pensée (pah^n **say**) thought; idea; reflection. Often used with reference to Pascal's *Pensées* (1670), a collection of aphorisms that includes the *aperçu* (which see), "I have discovered that all human evil comes from this, man's inability to sit still in a room."

perdu (pehr **dü**) lost; missing; confused; hopeless.

père (pehr) father; used after a name to distinguish father from son when they have the same name, as in "Alexandre Dumas, *père*."

Perfide Albion (pehr **feed** ahl bee yo^n) "Treacherous Albion," an anti-English Napoleonic recruiting slogan circa 1813.

persiflage (pehr see **flahzh**) raillery; light-hearted banter.

pétard (pay **tahr**) a small bomb or firecracker; a vulgar display; an intentionally shocking work of art. From the root *péter*, "to break wind." The *pétard*, a medieval bomb used to blow up gates or barricades, was notoriously unreliable, often killing or maiming the one employing it. Thus to be "hoist with one's own *pétard*" is to be defeated with one's own weapon or tactic.

> Let it work;
> For 'tis sport, to have the engineer
> Hoist with his own *pétard*; and it shall go hard
> But I will delve one yard below their mines,
> And blow them at the moon.

> —WILLIAM SHAKESPEARE, *Hamlet*, Act III, Scene 4

petit bourgeois (puh **tee** boor **zhwah**) the lower–middle class; a member of the lower–middle class.

> Spike Lee is a *petit bourgeois* who took the choice of selling his people for a fistful of dollars. Malcolm X was a revolutionary.
>
> —STOKELY CARMICHAEL, *International Herald Tribune*

petit déjeuner (puh **tee** day zhuh **nay**) "little lunch"; breakfast. The title of the French translation of Truman Capote's famous novel is *Petit déjeuner chez Tiffany*.

petite amie (puh **teet** ah **mee**) "little friend"; the young mistress of a middle-aged man.

petite maison (puh **teet** may **zo**^{n}) a small house or apartment maintained for a mistress.

petit four (puh **tee** **foor**) "small oven"; a decorative cookie or cake.

petit mort (puh **tee** **mohr**) "little death"; orgasm.

philosophe (**fee** loh **sohf**) a broad term for the scientists, writers, and thinkers of the eighteenth-century French Enlightenment, including Voltaire, Diderot, and Rousseau, who shared a belief in the supremacy of human reason.

> As Bill Clinton's choice for Secretary of Labor, [Robert] Reich has achieved Cabinet status. But even without portfolio he would be one of the most powerful people in town and, therefore, the world. Reich, perhaps more than any other contemporary *philosophe*, has exercised a profound influence on Elvis II's thinking since 1968, when the two young Rhodes scholars were sailing to England. Bob got seasick, Bill fetched chicken soup for him, and the two became fast friends.
>
> —ALAN PELL CRAWFORD, *ADWEEK*

pièce de résistance (**pyess** duh ray zees **tah**^{n}**s**) main dish; main attraction; the most important item in a group or collection.

> While a television camera hovers over her, Mrs. Kitaura prepares the *pièce de résistance*, ice cream sushi.
>
> —JUDITH OLNEY, *Washington Times*

pièce d'occasion (**pyess** doh kah **zyo**^{n}) a musical or literary work created for a special occasion.

pièce montée (**pyess** mo^n **tay**) "set piece"; a large, decorative dish, usually of pastry, reflecting the theme of special occasions such as weddings or baptisms.

pièce noire (pyess **nwahr**) "black piece." The playwright Jean Anouilh (1910–87) rejected the comedy/tragedy distinction and instead classified his plays as *pièces roses* (rosy pieces) or *pièces noires*.

pièce rose (pyess **rohz**) "rosy piece." See *pièce noire*.

pied à terre (**pyay** dah **tehr**) "foot on the ground"; a small apartment kept for convenience away from home.

pince nez (pa^{n}s **nay**) "pinch nose"; eyeglasses that clamp onto the nose.

piquant (pee **kah**^{n}) sharp, pointed; strong.

> It is good, in discourse and speech of conversation, to vary and intermingle speech of the present occasion with arguments, tales with reasons, asking of questions with telling of opinions, and jest with earnest: for it is a dull thing to tire, and, as we say now, to jade, any thing too far. As for jest, there be certain things which ought to be privileged from it; namely, religion, matters of state, great persons, any man's present business of importance, and any case that deserveth pity. Yet there be some that think their wits have been asleep, except they dart out somewhat that is *piquant*, and to the quick. That is a vein which would be bridled.
>
> —FRANCIS BACON, "Of Discourse"

pirouette (pee roo **wet**) "spinning top"; a ballet movement in which the body rotates on the point of the toe or ball of the foot.

pis aller (**pee** zah **lay**) the worst; the last resort.

planchette (plah^n **shet**) a small, triangular, Ouija board–like device used to summon supernatural forces.

> Into the face of the young man who sat on the terrace of
> the Hotel Magnifique at Cannes there had crept a look of
> furtive shame, the shifty, hangdog look which announces
> that an Englishman is about to talk French.
>
> —P. G. WODEHOUSE, *The Luck of the Bodkins*

plié (plee **yay**) a ballet position in which the dancer bends the
knees while his or her toes point outward.

plus ça change, plus c'est la même chose (plü sah **shahⁿzh**,
plü say lah mem **shohz**) "The more things [seem to] change,
the more they stay the same," often abbreviated as *plus ça
change* and bearing the sense of "I told you so!" The apho-
rism is usually attributed to the French journalist Alphonse
Karr (1808–90), who used it in 1849 to chastise the French
people for electing Louis-Napoléon Bonaparte president contrary to Karr's repeated warnings. He was vindicated two
years later when the president declared himself emperor.

> The Rehnquist court, absent further changes in personnel, with
> some minor exceptions, will not be as conservative as conserva-
> tives hope, and not as conservative as liberals fear. The same was
> true of the Burger court. With regard to the Rehnquist court the
> French adage seems fitting: *"Plus ça change, plus c'est la même
> chose."*
>
> —ARTHUR J. GOLDBERG, *Christian Science Monitor*

plus royaliste que le roi (reine) (plü rwah yah **leest** kuh luh
rwah [ren]) More royalist than the king (queen).

> It is difficult to date the moment when I first felt stirrings of
> interest in the colour of stamps, their themes, their cancellations;
> sensed pricklings of curiosity about postal history, and finally had
> a definite dislike of being an exile in my own household. The
> letters that arrived were mainly from France and Italy, and my
> love for these two countries drew me to their stamps. Through
> the letter box tumbled a whole panorama of French writers and
> artists, chateaux and cathedrals, Florentine and Venetian palaz-

zos, musicians of the Italian Baroque. What could not be learned from these pieces of paper!

As an aficionada I became *plus royaliste que le roi*. I dreamt those philatelic dreams of attics crammed with boxes of stamps, with forgeries and fabulous flaws. I eyed wastepaper baskets in post offices, for who knew what treasures might have been tossed into them carelessly, and I picked up stamps discarded on the village street.

—PIPPA STUART, *Christian Science Monitor*

poète maudit (poh et moh **dee**) "accursed poet"; one who is insufficiently appreciated by his contemporaries.

I swallowed Poe whole. Then I swallowed Hervey Allen's biography of Poe, *Israfel*, and discovered for myself the thrilling role of *poète maudit*. I wanted to grow up and be like Poe: I wanted to be mad, addicted, obsessed, haunted and cursed; I wanted to have deep eyes that burned like coals—profoundly melancholic, profoundly attractive.

—DONALD HALL, *New York Times*

point d'appui (pwa^n dah **pwee**) fulcrum; point of leverage.

Beyond Montgomery's endless stalling there was an anterior question: Why invade Italy? The invasion of Sicily had made sense largely in logistical terms: to open the Mediterranean and provide a *point d'appui* for attacks on, or major threats to, the only "soft underbelly" in Europe—the French coast from roughly Sète to Toulon.

—JOHN P. ROCHE, *National Review*

point d'honneur (pwa^n doh **nuhr**) point of honor.

pointillisme (pwa^n tee **yeez** muh) pointillism, a neo-impressionist style of painting whereby tiny dots are juxtaposed to form overall shape and color. *Pointillisme* is embodied in the work of its inventor and chief proponent, Georges Seurat (1859–91), whose *Un Dimanche d'été à la Grande Jatte* is the most famous example of the technique.

politesse (poh lee **tess**) politeness; good manners; exaggerated observance of etiquette.

I don't like Paris. And I don't like the French. This *politesse fran-çaise* gets on my nerves. Even when they are excessively nasty, they are excessively polite.

—EDITH TEMPLETON, *The New Yorker*

politique (poh lee **teek**) politics; political; politician.

pompier (pohmp **yay**) "pump maker"; a (wind) pumper; a fireman; a windbag; figuratively, one who "inhales" the style of another and "exhales" an imitation thereof, thus, also, a hackneyed style.

poseur (poh **zuhr**) one who affects a pose or attitude; one given to affectation.

Introduced in 1978, the 928 has always been a serious sporting machine. Yet its luxury fittings and versatile GT profile have earned it a reputation as something of a *poseur*'s Porsche, a car seen less often carving up mountain roads than being proudly handed over to the country-club valet.

—ARTHUR ST. ANTOINE, *Car and Driver*

poste restante (**pohst** res **tah^{n}t**) general (postal) delivery.

pot pourri (**poh** poo **ree**) "rotten pot"; a mixture of dried vegetable matter used to scent the air; a medley; a collection of diverse things.

pour encourager les autres (poor ah^n koo rah **zhay** lay **zoh** truh) "to encourage the others"; to make an example of someone. "Encourage" is used ironically, as in Voltaire's *Candide*: "It is a good thing to kill an admiral occasionally to encourage the others," an allusion to the execution of Admiral John Byng (1704–57) for his failure to break the French blockade of Minorca in 1756.

The young Saint-Just, who made several trips to the front, was capable of draconian acts of punishment if he discovered looting or other acts of military disorder on which his excessively tidy mind frowned. More than once he had delinquent officers cash-iered and shot in front of their own troops, *pour encourager les autres*.

—SIMON SCHAMA, *Citizens*

pourparler (poor pahr **lay**) discussions preliminary to a formal negotiation.

préciosité (pray syoh see **tay**) preciousness; affectation; over-refinement.

précis (**pray** see) a concise summary; an abstract.

prélude (**pray** lüd) a preliminary performance, action, or event; a short musical piece designed to foreshadow a longer composition.

première (pruh **myayr**) first performance; opening night.

prêt-à-porter (**preht** ah pohr **tay**) "off the peg"; ready-to-wear.

prix fixe (pree **feeks**) a menu on which the entire meal, from appetizer to dessert, is included in one fixed price. Synonymous with *table d'hôte* and the opposite *of à la carte*.

Prix Goncourt (**pree** go^n **koor**) a prestigious prize for French fiction awarded by the Académie Goncourt, a ten-member jury established in 1903 by the will of the French novelist Edmond de Goncourt (1822–96).

progressiste (proh gray **seest**) "progressive"; the opposite of *immobiliste* (which see).

(la) propriété, c'est le vol ([lah] proh pree ay **tay** say luh **vohl**) "Property is theft"; the opening statement of a treatise by the French social reformer Pierre-Joseph Proudhon (1809–65), which maintains that ownership of private property by some exploits the labor of others.

provocateur (proh **voh** kah **tuhr**) agitator; instigator.

Among the more interesting aspects of the ongoing culture war is the fact that the *avant-garde*, which one might have thought would be off the map by this late stage in the twentieth century, continues to cause problems. Robert Mapplethorpe, Bret Easton Ellis, Camille Paglia, Ice-T—such *provocateurs* have demonstrated that people are still ready to get worked up about art, literature, and aesthetics generally.

—RICHARD RYAN, *Commentary*

pudeur (pü **duhr**) sense of modesty or propriety.

puissance (pwee sah^{n}s) power; force; vigor.

> They were buoyed by love but powered by a lust as rich and demanding as their hale bodies deserved. Laura's teeth were bared as Rye drove into her with a *puissance* that soon set off the first pulsations deep within.
>
> —LA VYRLE SPENCER, *Twice Loved*

putain (poo ta^n) prostitute.

q

quart d'heure (kahr **duhr**) "quarter of an hour"; a one-act play.

quartier toléré (kahr **tyay** toh lay **ray**) a district in a city or town where brothels are officially tolerated.

quel dommage! (kel doh **mahz**) What a pity!

> What I want to know is: DID Tina Brown of the *New Yorker* only invite me out to lunch at the Four Seasons for "damage control" as the *News* says? *Quel dommage*! And here I thought she loved me as a friend and we were just gossiping in general.
>
> —LIZ SMITH, *Newsday*

quelque chose (**kel** kuh **shohz**) something; a trifle.

qui s'excuse s'accuse (kee seks küz **sah** küz) "He who excuses himself, accuses himself."

qui vive (kee **veev**) on the alert; watchful. One is "on the *qui vive*" when keeping a sharp lookout: The idiom descends from the sentry's challenge, *"Qui vive?"*, "(Long) live who?", i.e., who's side are you on? The proper royalist reply would have been, *"Vive le roi!,"* "Long live the king!"

Parlez-Vous Franglais?

~

The following words and phrases have been banned by the French linguistic inquisition:

accounting et planning, after-shave, le baby-sitter, le bar-maid, le beatnik, le best-seller, le blazer, les blue chips, le booking, le bookmaker, le boom, le boss, le bulldozer, bye-bye, le call girl, le camping, le cash-flow, le challenge, le checkout, le cheeseburger, les cliff-dwellers, le cockpit, le cocktail, le comeback, containment, le copyright, le cow-boy, le dancing, le drive-in, le drug store, le dumping, les chicken nuggets, le fast-food, fifty-fifty, le flashback, le gadget, le hamburger, le hijack, le hold-up, le hot dog, le jeans, le jingle, le job, le jogging, le jukebox, le jumbo jet, le kit, le know-how, les leaders, le look, le manager, le marketing, les meetings, le melting-pot, le name-dropping, le news desk, le new-wave, nonstop, le outsider, le park-ing, les pickpockets, le racket, le remake, rent-a-car, le rip off, le rock, le sandwich, le scoop, le self-made man, le shopping, le show-biz, le shuttle, soft-approach, le soft-ware, le snobbisme, le soda, le sponsor, le sportswear, les stars, les starting blocks, les streets, le stress, le supermar-ket, le venture capital, le weekend, le weekend sexy, le zapping, zoom.

r

raconteur (rah ko^n **tuhr**) a skilled storyteller.

raison d'état (ray **zo^n** day **tah**) "reason of state"; the doctrine that the interests of a nation transcend moral considerations, which is frequently offered as an excuse for a government's bad behavior.

> There's no colder phrase in diplomacy than *raison d'état*, the justification that enables decent people to do the indecent for flag and country.
>
> —KARL E. MEYER, *New York Times*

raison d'être (ray **zo^n deh** truh) "reason for being"; justification; rationale.

> The organization [Association Amicale des Amateurs d'Authentiques Andouillettes], founded in the late 1950's by the legendary critic Robert Courtine, acquires new panel members only as members die, something like the United States Supreme Court. Its *raison d'être* is to bestow baroquely festooned certificates on those restaurants and producers that make the best-tasting tripe sausage.
>
> —DAVID ROSENGARTEN, *New York Times*

raisonné (ray zo^n **nay**) well reasoned; rational; logical.

raisonneur (ray zo^n **nuhr**) "reasoner"; a character in a play or novel, often a confidant of the protagonist, who comments on the action.

rappel (rah **pehl**) to descend a steep cliff by means of a double rope; from *rappeler*, to summon or recall.

rapprochement (rah prohsh **mah^n**) a coming together; a reestablishment of friendly relations, especially between nations.

réchauffé (**ray** shoh **fay**) "warmed over"; rehashed; stale; hackneyed.

> That piece, sandwiched between Shaker Loops and Grand Pianola Music, proved the low point. Inspired by the music of Takemitsu, it shows Adams' powers of construction at their weakest, and its language of Skryabin, Berg and Messiaen *réchauffé* at his flabbiest.
>
> —DAVID MURRAY and ANDREW CLEMENTS, *Financial Times* (London)

recherché (ruh shehr **shay**) sought after; choice; in great demand; exotic; exquisite; affected.

> After a few minutes of home movies showing Cher's evolution from infant to multimedia goddess, she sauntered out to the sanitized heavy-metal beat of "I'm No Angel" (Costume No. 1: *recherché* torn jeans, short rhinestone jacket, which she removed— No. 2).
>
> —JOE BROWN, *Washington Post*

régime (ray **zheem**) a form of government; the government in power; a regimen of diet, exercise, therapy, etc. designed to improve health.

règle du jeu (**rehg** luh dü **zhuh**) rules of the game.

rendezvous (rahⁿ day **voo**) a meeting place; a prearranged meeting at a designated place; an assembly point. The origin is military: The order *"Rendez vous,"* "Present yourselves," was used to marshal troops and other forces as far back as the late sixteenth century.

rentier (rahⁿ **tyay**) one who lives off investments; a "coupon-clipper."

> I used to dislike Florence, its inadequate river, its medieval bankers' machicolated fortresses miscalled palaces, its inadequately Mediterranean climate and rainy *rentier* reminders of Bath and Cheltenham.
>
> —CYRIL CONNOLLY, "The Grand Tour"

renversement (rahⁿ vehrs **mahⁿ**) reversal of fortune.

répétiteur (ray **pay** tee **tuhr**) "repeater"; a musical director or vocal coach; a prompter or tutor.

répondez s'il vous plaît (ray po^n **day** seel voo **play**) "Reply, if you please." Often abbreviated *RSVP*.

(la) république des lettres ([lah] ray püb **leek** duh **leh** truh) "(the) republic of letters"; the commonwealth of literati.

(la) Résistance ([lah] **ray** zees **tah^{n}s**) an organization of French guerrilla fighters during World War II, also known as the *maquis*.

restaurateur (res toh rah **tuhr**) the proprietor of a restaurant.

retroussé (reh troo **say**) turned up.

> The pet girl of the convent was a fragile Jewish girl named Susie Lowenstein, who had pale red-gold hair and an exquisite *retroussé* nose, which, if we had had it, might have been called "pug."
>
> —MARY MCCARTHY, *Memories of a Catholic Girlhood*

revanche (ruh **vah^{n}sh**) revenge, especially political, e.g., the desire of a nation to regain lost territory or status, as in France's policy toward Alsace and Lorraine between 1871 and 1919.

revanchisme (ruh vah^n **sheez** muh) a policy based on the desire for political revenge.

revanchiste (ruh vah^n **sheest**) one who advocates *revanche*, e.g., vengeful measures against a defeated enemy.

> Although [Willy Brandt] clung to the nebulous goal of "unity of the nation" (a term he distinguished from "reunification," which he rejected because of its *revanchiste* overtones), he cajoled his countrymen to come to terms with the legacy of Hitler.
>
> —DAVID MARSH, *Financial Times* (London)

revenant (ruh vuh **nah^n**) one who returns from a long exile; one who returns from the dead; a ghost; an apparition.

revenons à nos moutons (ruh vuh **no**ⁿ zah noh moo **to**ⁿ) "Let us return to our sheep"; let's get back to the subject at hand. This proverbial expression is a quotation from a court scene in a medieval farce, *La Farce de Maître Pathelin*, in which the confused judge keeps urging the litigants to stick to the issue at hand, the ownership of a flock of sheep.

révolté (**ray** vohl **tay**) rebel; nonconformist.

rien ne va plus (ree yeⁿ nuh vah **plü**) "No more bets"; the *croupier*'s warning to players at the roulette wheel.

risqué (rees **kay**) suggestive of impropriety; off-color.

rococo (roh **koh** koh) an ornate decorative arts style that reached its height during the reign of Louis XV (1715–74), characterized by shell and foliage motifs and exemplified in the furniture and architecture of the Versailles palace. Its more flamboyant examples have made the term *rococo* indicative of pretension and tastelessness. From *rocaille*, "rockwork."

roi fainéant (rwah **fay** nay **ah**ⁿ) "do-nothing king"; an impotent leader; a figurehead.

> The damage inflicted upon Louis XVI by Marie Antoinette and upon Nicholas II by the Empress Alexandra is now being visited upon Clinton, the hapless *roi fainéant,* by his appalling wife and the coven of Hollywood harpies and Barbie Dolls from hell who are presently demolishing what remains of American greatness and decency.
>
> —GERALD WARNER, *Sunday Times* (London)

(le) roi le veut ([luh] **rwah** luh **vuh**) (The) king wills it.

(le) roi s'amuse ([luh] **rwah** sah **müz**) (The) king is amused.

(le) roi s'avisera ([luh] **rwah** sah vee **zrah**) (The) king will consider it.

Roi Soleil (rwah soh **lay**) "Sun King"; the nickname for Louis Quatorze (which see).

roman à cléf (roh **mah**ⁿ nah **klay**) "novel with a key"; a novel in which real persons are disguised as fictional characters.

[*Degree of Guilt* by Richard North Patterson] opens with Mary Carelli, America's most famous television journalist, alone in a hotel room with the half-naked body of Mark O'Malley Ransom, America's most famous writer. Ransom is very dead indeed—the question is, did he rape her?—and immediately the *roman à cléf* cleaves to our brains: Would Barbara Walters do this to Norman Mailer?

—SIDNEY ZION, *New York Times*

roman à tiroirs (roh **mah**ⁿ ah teer **wahr**) "novel with drawers"; a novel consisting of ostensibly unconnected episodes.

roman fleuve (roh **mah**ⁿ **fluhv**) "river novel"; a series of novels chronicling the same characters, such as Balzac's *La Comédie humaine*, Zola's *Les Rougon-Macquart*, or Galsworthy's *The Forsyte Saga*.

If you're counting, *Very Old Bones* is the seventh work in which William Kennedy writes of his native city, the sixth novel in his Albany cycle—a generational saga of civic and family history, a *roman fleuve*, if you will, the lordly Hudson being the only river in view.

—MAUREEN HOWARD, *New York Times*

roman noir (roh **mah**ⁿ **nwahr**) "black novel"; the term applied to nineteenth-century English gothic novels, and later to the hardboiled fiction of such novelists as Cornell Woolrich and Jim Thompson, the literary forerunners of *film noir* (which see).

"Shoot the Piano Player" (1962), Francois Truffaut's tragicomedy of a concert pianist slumming in a Paris café . . . [is] the first of the director's stabs at that peculiarly French preoccupation, the *roman noir*—seamy and compellingly fatalistic sagas of American lowlife.

—STEVE DOLLAR, *Atlanta Journal and Constitution*

rondeau (roⁿ **doh**) "round"; a verse form consisting of thirteen or fifteen lines in three stanzas.

roseau pensant (roh **zoh** paⁿ **sah**ⁿ) "thinking reed." *Pensées* (1670), a collection of epigrams by the philosopher Blaise Pascal (1623–62), includes an oft-quoted observation on the human race: *"L'homme n'est qu'un roseau, le plus faible de la nature, mais c'est un roseau pensant,"* "Man is only a reed, the weakest in nature, but he is a thinking reed."

rossignol (roh see **nyohl**) nightingale.

roué (roo **ay**) a lecher; a rake; from *rouer*, "to turn a wheel, to be turned upon a wheel." A *roué* is thus a profligate who literally deserves to be tortured on the wheel, a punishment reserved for the most heinous of criminals in eighteenth-century France. The duc d'Orléans maintained a hand-picked palace guard which he dubbed his *roués* because, he said, every one of them deserved to be broken on the wheel. The *roués* accepted the name, but claimed that it described their loyalty to the duke; they would, if necessary, allow themselves to be broken on the wheel in his service.

> Americans, to judge from the movies they make and attend, are fast, rough, raunchy lovers—backseat studs and born-to-thrill prom queens. Canadians cannot decide whether to imitate American energy or British reserve. Germans are dogmatic and ironic by turns; and the men snore in bed, but only, as one of them explains, "to protect their women from wild animals." As for the French, who didn't invent love but certainly know how to market it, they negotiate their affairs with a *roué*'s smile and a fatalist's shrug. *C'est l'amour. C'est la vie.*
>
> —RICHARD CORLISS, *Time*

ruse de guerre (rüz duh **gehr**) stratagem of war.

> The incident of the Trojan Horse, even if it is to be regarded as a mythical archetype rather than a historical event, was no more than a successful *ruse de guerre*, a single if disastrous example of misjudgment.
>
> —MICHAEL HOWARD, *Washington Post*

S

sabotage (**sah** boh **tahzh**) malicious destruction of property, or disruption of normal operations of an enemy or competitor; deliberate subversion. A word with a long history and disagreement about its origin. No one doubts its root: *sabot*, a type of shoe or clog fashioned from a single piece of wood (and therefore not of fine workmanship). In the nineteenth century, disgruntled workers used their *sabots* to destroy manufactured goods like fine cloth, or to "clog" machinery. On the other hand, the first *saboteurs* may have been peasants who trampled their crops (with their sabots) in protest against their feudal masters. In any case, the word did not gain currency in English until the early twentieth century, when French workers sabotaged rail operations during a strike.

sang froid (sah^n **fwah**) "cold blood"; poise; composure; self-possession.

> Let what will be said or done, preserve your *sang froid* immovably, and to every obstacle, oppose patience, perseverance, and soothing language.
>
> —THOMAS JEFFERSON, letter to William Short

sans (sah^n) without.

> Last scene of all,
> That ends this strange eventful history,
> Is second childishness and mere oblivion,
> *Sans* teeth, *sans* eyes, *sans* taste, *sans* every thing.
>
> —WILLIAM SHAKESPEARE, *As You Like It*, Act II, Scene 7

sans culottes (sah^n kü **loht**) "without breeches"; the nickname for prerevolutionary tradesmen and artisans who defiantly wore ordinary trousers instead of the knee breeches of the aristocracy. The term is now applied to any radical or militant.

> In the days of Proposition 13 in the late '70s, California had an image of suntanned taxpayers *sans culottes* revolting against government levies on their hard-won lifestyle.
>
> —SUSAN MOFFAT, *Los Angeles Times*

sans façon (sah^n fah so^n) without ceremony; informal.

> Reading about Mozart's personal life we recognise that he was informal, to say the least, *sans façon*. He struck no attitudes— the very idea of "genius" was alien to him.
>
> —SAUL BELLOW, *Guardian*

sans pareil (sah^n pah rehl) without equal.

sans peur et sans reproche (sah^n puhr ay sah^n ruh prohsh) "Without fear and without reproach"; chivalrous.

> Whether Winston Churchill was the immaculate patron saint of the bulldog breed, *chevalier sans peur et sans reproche*, or a self-seeking pseud who got lucky, is a debate for the historians and the pseudo-historians.
>
> —PHILIP HOWARD, *Times* (London)

sans phrase (sah^n frahz) straight out; without mincing words.

> In 1793, during the trial of Louis XVI, members of the French Convention delivered impassioned and eloquent speeches on the proposal to execute the king. Finally, the Abbé Sieyes stood up and offered his opinion: *"La mort, sans phrase."* Death, without discussion. The same thing happened in the Senate Finance Committee last week.
>
> —WILLIAM SCHNEIDER, *Los Angeles Times*

sans souci (sah^n soo see) without worry; carefree.

sauté (soh tay) to fry in a pan with butter, fat, or oil; a dish so prepared.

sauve qui peut (sohv kee puh) "Save himself who can"; every man for himself.

> A nation which dispatches an aircraft carrier to the Gulf war without any aeroplanes appears driven by principles which are

unchanging. There seems no nationality with whom it is less advisable to be competing for a place in a lifeboat after a shipwreck than the originators of *sauve qui peut*. This is what creates the despair of Eurocrats. We enjoy hating and distrusting the French, just as they enjoy reciprocating our sentiments, with interest.

—*Daily Telegraph* (London)

savoir-faire (sahv wahr **fehr**) "knowing how to do"; the ability to do the right thing no matter what the circumstances; self-assurance; poise.

[Alex] Trebek's on-camera *savoir-faire* didn't always carry over to his personal life. During one show three years ago, after a contestant correctly guessed that flamingos mate just once a year, Trebek, divorced in 1981 after a childless seven-year marriage, ad-libbed, "Flamingos and I have a great deal in common."

—KRISTINA JOHNSON, *People*

savoir-plaindre (sah vwahr **pla**^{n} druh) "knowing how to complain."

Like Rabelais, Villon, Baudelaire and Corbière before him, Céline was an incomparable complainer. Though the French are celebrated for their *savoir-vivre*, their finest talent is for *savoir-plaindre*. They can never forgive Descartes for having dangled before their eyes a dream of reason in an unreasonable world. No one has ever raised ruefulness to such inspired heights as the French, and the falling off of their literature today can be partly traced to the virtual loss of that ruefulness. Céline was the last of the grand vituperators, a gourmet of disgust. He reminded us that in French the word *degout* is almost onomatopoeic.

—ANATOLE BROYARD, *New York Times*

savoir-vivre (sahv wahr **vee** vruh) "knowing how to live"; good manners; social grace; tact.

scène à faire (**sen** ah **fehr**) an obligatory scene; a standard plot device.

secrétaire (**suh** kray **tehr**) "secretary"; writing desk with top section for books.

(le) secret de Polichinelle ([luh] suh **kray** duh poh lee shee **nel**) an open secret. Polichinelle was a seventeenth-century French puppet (the prototype of Mr. Punch of the Punch and Judy shows) whose secrets were told in stage whispers.

> Mitterrand has had sexual trysts with well-known female journalists who appear frequently on television to comment on his presidency. And Giscard's liaison with a well-known actress is another *secret de Polichinelle*.
>
> —MATTHEW FRASER, *Montreal Gazette*

si jeunesse savait, si vieillesse pouvait (see zhuh **ness** sah vay see **vyay** ess poo vay) If the young only knew, if the old only could.

s'il vous plaît (seel voo **play**) if you please.

simpliste (sam **pleest**) simplistic; superficial.

> What's the French for fiddle-de-dee?
> —LEWIS CARROLL, *Alice's Adventures in Wonderland*

---

sobriquet (soh bree **kay**) nickname; pseudonym.

soi-disant (swah dee **zah**^{n}) self-styled; pretended.

> In those days, an abductee named Buck Nelson sold little packets of fur at $5 each, which he said came from a Venusian Saint Bernard weighing 385 pounds. Another *soi-disant* contactee, Howard Menger, explained on the "Tonight" show how easy it was to breathe on the moon and subsequently cut a record entitled "The Song From Saturn"—which ditty, he averred, was "actual music that came from another planet."
>
> —CURT SUPLEE, *Washington Post*

soigné (swahn **yay**) tidy; neat; well groomed; elegantly simple.

> Whatever our differences, we can always swap tips on hair, clothes and makeup, the way fathers and sons talk sports. And I don't have to waste a lot of time reading fashion magazines. Mother, *soignée* to the fourth power, has the beauty equivalent of the Rand Corporation on call.
>
> —MARGO KAUFMAN, *New York Times Magazine*

soirée (swah **ray**) "evening"; an evening party.

sommelier (soh mel **yay**) wine waiter.

son et lumière (**so**^{n} ay lü **myehr**) "sound and light"; spectacle and pageantry presented at night, usually in an ancient or dramatic setting, featuring music, fireworks, and flood-lighting.

sortie (sohr **tee**) exit; a military mission or attack; a venturing forth. From *sortir*, "to go out." The early meaning involved a breakout by a besieged or surrounded military force, but the word has come to connote a specific combat mission by a single warplane.

sou (soo) a five-centime piece; any coin of little value.

soubrette (soo **bret**) the part of a saucy maidservant in comic theater; an actress who plays such a part; a flirtatious young woman. From the Provençal *soubreto*, "conceited."

soubriquet (soo bree **kay**) see *sobriquet.*

soupçon (soop **so**^{n}) "suspicion"; a very small amount; in cooking, a "pinch."

(le) style, c'est l'homme (même) ([luh] **steel** say **lohm** [mehm]) "The style is the man (himself)," a quotation from *Discours sur le Style* (1753) by the French naturalist Georges-Louis Le-clerc, Comte de Buffon (1707–88).

> Rejection and acceptance, encouragement and tougher forms of counsel are, of course, central to the publishing process. The nature of what one accepts, the blindness—or vision—with which one rejects: all reveal the editor as surely as *le style c'est l'homme* (or *la femme*).
>
> —NICK LYONS, *New York Times*

succès de scandale (sük **say** duh skah^n **dahl**) "scandalous success"; success due to the notoriety accompanying a work or performance.

> Before his Oscar haul, Bertolucci's best-known film in this country was *Last Tango in Paris*, the *succès de scandale* starring Marlon Brando and Maria Schneider as the parties to a rather

unconventional love affair. Many were amazed to discover that a man and a woman could get so much done without taking any clothes off.

—TERRY KELLEHER, *Newsday*

succès d'estime (sük **say** day **steem**) "honorable success"; a critical success but a commercial failure.

We could all learn something from Brown, Kerrey and Tsongas. But who's really listening? In politics, a *succès d'estime* is no success at all—just ask Adlai Stevenson.

—ALEX BEAM, *Boston Globe*

succès fou (sük **say** foo) "wild success"; a smash hit.

sûreté (sür **tay**) security; safety.

(la) Sûreté ([lah] sür **tay**) the French criminal investigation department (home of the bungling Inspector Clouseau in the *Pink Panther* movies).

sur le vif (sür luh **veef**) lifelike.

sur place (sür **plahss**) on the spot.

tableau (tah **bloh**) picture; painting.

tableau vivant (tah **bloh** vee **vah**ⁿ) "living picture"; a representation of a scene by motionless persons, i.e., in "suspended animation."

table d'hôte (**tah** bluh **doht**) the regular menu of a restaurant; a fixed-price meal (as opposed to *à la carte*).

tachisme (tah **sheez** muh) action painting; a technique in which the artist applies splotches of paint to a canvas apparently at random. From *tache*, "stain."

tant mieux (tah**ⁿ myuh**) So much the better.

tant pis (tah**ⁿ pee**) So much the worse; it can't be helped.

> *Tant pis* and *tant mieux*, being two of the great hinges in French conversation, a stranger would do well to set himself right in the use of them before he gets to Paris.
>
> —LAURENCE STERNE, *A Sentimental Journey*

tartuffe (tahr **tüf**) a hypocrite. After the two-faced title character of a Molière play.

tendresse (tah**ⁿ dress**) tenderness; affection.

terre à terre (tehr ah **tehr**) down to earth; a series of ballet steps in which the feet barely leave the ground.

tête à tête (tet ah **tet**) "head to head"; two alone together; a private conversation between two persons.

tête bêche (**tet besh**) "top to bottom"; a pair of postage stamps one of which is upside down in relation to the other.

texte intégral (tekst a**ⁿ** tay **grahl**) complete text; unabridged version.

Tiers État (**tyehr** zay **tah**) "Third Estate"; the common legislative body of prerevolutionary France.

toilette (twah **let**) the process of grooming or dressing; a person's clothing or style of dress.

(la) toque blanche ([lah] tohk **blahnsh**) "(the) white hat"; the familiar French chef's tall white hat.

touché (too **shay**) in fencing, the announcement of a touch or hit; in conversation, the acknowledgment of a stinging remark.

toujours de l'audace! (too **zhoor** duh loh **dahss**) "Daring always pays!" On September 2, 1792, the acting minister of justice Georges-Jacques Danton (1759–94) rallied Paris against the Prussian invasion with a stirring speech to the National Assembly that ended with the rousing cry, *"De l'audace, et encore de l'audace, et toujours de l'audace!"*

toujours la politesse (too **zhoor** lah poh lee **tess**) Politeness always pays.

toujours perdrix (too **zhoor** pehr **dree**) "always partridge"; too much of a good thing.

> Last night's Opening Ceremonies of the XVI Olympic Winter Games was thoroughly French—a mix of *avant-garde* and traditional, creating an elaborate sensory overload. It aimed for childlike craziness, coupled with unrestrained imagination, and hit its mark—over and over and over. *Toujours perdrix.*
>
> —JOHN JEANSONNE, *Newsday*

tour de force (toor duh **fors**) feat of strength; display of skill.

> Through all these controversies, [Hans-Dietrich] Genscher maneuvered with consummate skill. History will surely record as his monument the *tour de force* of unifying his country while sustaining Germany's Atlantic relationships.
>
> —HENRY A. KISSINGER, *Newsweek*

(le) Tour de France ([luh] toor duh **frah**^{n}**s**) an annual two-week bicycle race around France.

toujours perdrix

tour d'horizon (toor dohr ee zo^n) "circuit of the horizon"; general survey.

Sitting before a portrait of George Washington, Bush referred to a stack of 3-by-5 cards as he gave Clinton a ***tour d'horizon*** of the world's hot spots, including Russia, the former Yugoslavia and the Middle East. The 68-year-old president's message to his 46-year-old successor: No matter how much you try to focus on domestic issues, the world always intrudes.

—KENNETH T. WALSH, *U.S. News & World Report*

tout à l'heure (too tah luhr) presently; just now.

tout au contraire (too toh ko^n trehr) quite the contrary.

tout à vous (too tah voo) all yours; at your service; sincerely yours.

tout comprendre c'est tout pardonner (too kohm pra^n druh say too pahr do^n nay) To understand all is to forgive all.

The relations between knowing and judging are complicated; the empirical and the moral cannot be easily disentangled. It is not always true that *tout comprendre c'est tout pardonner*. Comprehension does not always lead to forgiveness. In certain cases, indeed, forgiveness may signify the absence of comprehension.

—LEON WIESELTIER, *The New Republic*

tout de même (tood **mem**) all the same; nevertheless.

tout de suite (tood **sweet**) all at once; immediately.

tout ensemble (too tah^n **sahm** bluh) all together; the general effect.

tout est perdu hors l'honneur (too tay pehr **dü** ohr loh **nuhr**) "All is lost except honor"; French king François I (1494–1547), informing his mother of his defeat at Pavia (1525).

tout est pour le mieux dans le meilleur des mondes possibles (too tay poor luh **myuh** dah^n luh **may** yuhr day **mo^{n}d** poh **see** bluh) "All is for the best in the best of all possible worlds," the oft-repeated philosophy of Doctor Pangloss in Voltaire's *Candide*. See also, *Pangloss*.

tout frais faits (**too** fray **fay**) all expenses paid.

tout le monde (**too** luh **mo^{n}d**) all the world; everyone.

tranche de vie (**trah^{n}sh** duh vee) "slice of life"; a dramatic representation of "real life" unadulterated by artifice.

triage (tree **ahzh**) a means of classifying injured people on the basis of their need for, and potential benefit from, immediate medical treatment; a system for allocating scarce commodities. From *trier*, "to sort."

Tricolore (tree koh **lohr**) "tricolor"; the red, white, and blue flag of the French Republic.

tristesse (treest **ess**) melancholy; depression.

Today we deal with post-Oscar *tristesse*. That's the remorse experienced when, having sat up all night watching the Academy Awards, people wake next morning realizing they hadn't seen half the movies in the competition, hadn't heard of most of the actors, can't remember who won a single Oscar last year, and don't give a hoot who won last night.

—RUSSELL BAKER, *New York Times*

Tristesse Verlainienne (treest ess vehr len yen) the lyrical melancholy typical of the poetry of Paul Verlaine (1844–96).

(les) trois coups ([lay] twah koo) "(the) three knocks" originally given as a warning just before the curtain rose at the Comédie Française (which see), and a standard practice in all French theaters (and even in amateur productions of French plays in American schools).

trompe l'oeil (trohmp loy) "deception of the eye"; optical illusion; artistic or decorative sham.

To some, [William M.] Harnett . . . was the American Zeuxis, the Greek painter (none of whose works survive) who was said to be so good at ***trompe l'oeil*** that birds flew down to peck the grapes in one of his still lifes, thus proving that he could bamboozle not only men but Nature herself.

—ROBERT HUGHES, *Time*

trousseau (troo soh) clothing and other items acquired by a young woman in anticipation of marriage. From the Old French *trousse*, "bundle."

truffe (trüf) truffle, a rare subterranean fungus valued as a great delicacy.

Brillat-Savarin says that the ***truffe*** is the diamond of the kitchen; that it awakens erotic and gourmand memories in the skirted sex, and gourmand and erotic souvenirs in the bearded sex. The ***truffe*** is certainly not a positive aphrodisiac, but in certain circumstances it can make women more tender, and men more amiable.

—ALEXANDRE DUMAS, père, *Grand Dictionnaire de Cuisine*

tulipe noire (tü leep nwahr) "black tulip"; a unique thing; an oddity.

V

ventre à terre (vah^n truh ah **tehr**) "belly to the ground"; at full speed.

vérité (vay ree **tay**) truth.

vers de société (**vehr** duh soh **see** ay **tay**) light, often satirical verse dealing with current affairs.

vers libre (vehr **lee** bruh) free verse.

(le) vice anglais ([luh] **veehs** ah^n **glay**) "(the) English vice." There it is: the French suspect the English of inventing the "vice" of homosexuality. And their dim view of English morals isn't confined to the bedroom: *anglais* is made a verb in the nasty little idiom, *anglaiser quelqu'un*, "to cheat someone." The disdain is mutual: *French* is a metaphor for much of what English speakers find naughty or perverse about sex. Thus "French postcards," "French letters" (condoms), the "French pox" (syphilis), and the standard apology for profanity, "Pardon my French."

> Did you know what *le vice anglais* . . . really is? Not flagellation, not pederasty—whatever the French believe it to be. It's our refusal to admit our emotions. We think they demean us, I suppose.
>
> —TERENCE RATTIGAN, *In Praise of Love*

vichyssoise (vee shee **swahz**) cold potato soup.

vie amoureuse (vee ah moor **uhz**) "love life"; sexual history.

(la) vie de Bohème ([lah] **veed** boh **ehm**) (the) Bohemian life; the unconventional lifestyle of artists, writers, actors, and musicians.

vie manquée (vee mah^n **kay**) misdirected life; a life spent in the wrong profession.

vieux jeu (vyuh **zhuh**) old hat; out of date.

ville lumière (**veel** lüm **yehr**) city of light, i.e., Paris. The name may go back to 1470, when the first book to issue from the first printing press in France, *Receuil des lettres de Gasparin de Bergame*, was dedicated to Paris for its physical radiance and cultural brilliance.

vinaigrette (va^n ay **gret**) a dish prepared or served with a vinegar sauce; a small bottle or box designed to hold aromatic spirits.

vin blanc (va^n **blah^{n}k**) white wine.

vin du pays (va^n dü pay ee) wine of the region.

vin ordinaire (va^n ohr dee **nehr**) table wine.

vin rouge (va^n **roozh**) red wine.

vis-à-vis (vee zah **vee**) "face to face"; opposite; relative to. From an old carriage or coach in which passengers sat facing one another.

vive la différence! (**veev** lah dee fay **rah^{n}s**) "Long live the difference!" (between men and women). The ultimate Gallicism.

vive la reine! (**veev** lah **ren**) Long live the queen!

vive le roi! (**veev** luh **rwah**) Long live the king!

vogue la galère (**vohg** lah gah **lehr**) "Let the galley keep going"; keep on no matter what; go for it! The phrase is sometimes attributed to Rabelais (1494?–1553?) but is actually an old proverb.

voilà (vwah **lah**) Behold!; there it is! Often used to simultaneously call attention to, and express satisfaction with, a given accomplishment, as in, "Now blend the heavy cream with the butter and the egg yolks and *voilà*, coronary-on-a-plate!"

volte face (**vohlt** fahss) "about face"; reversal of attitude; complete turnaround.

The Axis was an astonishingly loose alliance, with no specific, contractual obligations. Tokyo was not informed of the wheeling

and dealing over the German-Soviet Non-Aggression Pact—the
sudden *volte face* which precipitated World War II—nor fore-
warned of the German invasion of Russia.

—ALISTAIR HORNE, *National Review*

volupté (voh lüp **tay**) voluptuousness; sensual pleasure.

vouloir, c'est pouvoir (voo **lwahr** say poo **vwahr**) Where
there's a will there's a way.

Voyage à Cythère (vwah **yahzh** ah see **tehr**) "Journey to Cy-
thera," the island home of Aphrodite, Greek goddess of love,
and hence a quest for erotic experience. From the title of a
poem by Baudelaire.

voyage imaginaire (vwah **yahzh** ee mah zhee **nehr**) imaginary
journey.

Whene'er I hear French spoken as I approve
I find myself quietly falling in love.
              —E. R. BULWER-LYTTON, *Lucile*, 1860

---

voyant (vwah **yah**[n]) "seer"; a psychic.

voyeur (vwah **yuhr**) one who derives obsessive pleasure from
watching sexual activity; a peeping Tom.

vue d'ensemble (vü dah[n] **sahm** bluh) overall view.

vulgarisateur (vül **gah** ree zah **tuhr**) popularizer; one who
writes on technical subjects for the general public. Synonymous with *animateur*.

Z

zut alors! (züt ah **lohr**) an exclamation of disgust or exasperation.

Noms de lieu
~

Alsace-Lorraine (ahl **sahs** loh **ren**) a region of eastern France on the French/German border that has been the object of constant dispute between the two nations. Now under French rule, it was annexed by Germany in 1871 and again in 1940, and returned to France at the end of World War II.

Ardennes (ahr **den**) a region of lakes and forests in northern France where the Battle of the Bulge was fought during World War II.

Arles (ahrl) a Provençal town on the left bank of the Rhône where Vincent van Gogh painted some of his greatest works, including *Sunflowers, Starry Night,* and *The Bridge at Arles.*

(la) Bastille ([lah] bahs **tee**) a fourteenth-century fortress in Paris where political enemies of the monarchy were imprisoned. It was attacked on July 14, 1789, by an angry mob who captured its stores of ammunition, killed its governor, and released its inmates. The sacking of the Bastille, regarded by the French citizenry as a symbol of tyranny (though only seven prisoners were confined there at the time), sparked the French Revolution, and July 14th has since been celebrated as the foremost French holiday.

Bohème (boh **ehm**) "Bohemia," figuratively, the natural habitat of gypsies and artists, literally, a region of Czechoslovakia.

Bois de Boulogne (**bwah** duh boo **lohn** yuh) a park and recreational area in Paris containing the racetracks Longchamp and Auteuil.

Bordeaux (bohr **doh**) a commercial seaport and industrial city in southwestern France famous for its wines.

Bordeaux is . . . dedicated to the worship of Bacchus in the most discreet form.

—HENRY JAMES, *A Little Tour in France*

(la) Bourse ([lah] boors) "purse"; the Paris stock exchange, established in 1724.

Burgundy (boor gun dee) a region in eastern France known for its eponymous wines.

Calvados (kahl vah **dohs**) a *département* in Normandy where a distinctive apple brandy is produced.

Cannes (kahn) a resort city on the Mediterranean coast of France famous for its beautiful beaches and annual film festival.

Cap d'Antibes (kahp dah^n **teeb**) a noted winter resort on the Mediterranean coast near Nice.

(Saint Jean) Cap Ferrat ([sa^n zhah^n] **kahp** fay **rah**) a resort and seaport in the southeast of France near Nice.

Champagne (shahm **pahn** yuh) a province in northeastern France where an eponymous sparkling white wine is produced.

(le) Champ de Mars ([luh] shah^n duh **mahr**) "Field of Mars"; a large field on the Left Bank of the Seine in Paris that was once used as a parade ground.

Champs-Élysées (sha^n zeh lee **zay**) "Elysian Fields"; the world's most famous boulevard, connecting two Parisian landmarks, the Arc de Triomphe and the Place de la Concorde.

Cognac (kohn yahk) a city in western France where cognac is produced.

Compiègne (kohm **pyehn**) a town in northern France where the armistice of 1918 was signed, and where

Adolf Hitler received France's surrender to Germany in June 1940.

***Côte d'Azur* (koht** dah **zhür)** "Azure Coast," the Mediterranean coast of France; also known as the French Riviera.

***Côte d'Or* (koht dohr)** the "Gold Coast" of southern France.

***Deauville* (doh** veel) a famous beach resort and horse-racing center on the northwestern coast of France.

***Dordogne* (dohr dohn** yuh) a *département* in southwestern France known for its prehistoric artifacts and cave paintings.

***Fontainebleau* (fo^n** ten **bluh)** a town near Paris famous for its royal palace.

***France D'Outremer* (frah^{n}s** doo truh **mehr)** "Overseas France"; a loose union of former French colonies.

***Lourdes* (loord)** a small town at the foot of the Pyrénées in southwestern France where a peasant girl named Bernadette Soubirous reported a vision of the Virgin Mary. Lourdes is now the site of a Roman Catholic shrine where miraculous cures are believed to occur.

> At the end of the information given about a town in the guide-book, you often find a mention of its specialty. For ***Lourdes***, it says: "*Spécialité: Chocolat.*"
>
> —JAMES THURBER, *My World and Welcome to It*

***(le) Louvre* ([luh] loo** vruh) the national art gallery and museum of France, located in Paris. The Louvre palace, the single largest building in Paris and the largest museum in the world, was built in the sixteenth century by King François I (1494–1547), who began the art collection with works by Da Vinci, Raphael, and Titian. The collection was greatly expanded by Louis XIV (1638–1715), who also renovated the building. The legendary Louvre is the world's foremost repository of fine art, housing over 400,000 works, including the *Mona Lisa, Venus de Milo, Winged Victory of Samothrace,* and masterpieces by Michelangelo, Cranach, Botticelli, David, Vermeer, Rubens, Delacroix, Fragonard, Ingres, and Manet. A controversial glass pyramid and underground mall designed by I. M. Pei was commissioned by President François Mitterand and completed in 1989.

> I never knew what a palace was until I had a glimpse of the **Louvre**.
>
> —NATHANIEL HAWTHORNE

Marseille (mahr **say**) an industrial city and major seaport in southeastern France.

Montmartre (mo^n **mahr** truh) a district on the Right Bank of Paris noted for its nightlife and bohemian atmosphere.

Montparnasse (mo^n pahr **nahss**) a quarter in south-central Paris and a center of student and artistic life.

Nice (nees) A seaport in southeastern France and the leading resort on the French Riviera.

Normandy (nohr mah^n **dee**) A region of northwestern France on the English Channel and the site of the Allied invasion of Europe on June 6, 1944.

Notre Dame (**noh** truh **dahm**) "Our Lady," i.e., the Virgin Mary; the name of one of the most famous cathedrals in the world, located in Paris.

Père Lachaise (**pehr** lah **shez**) a Parisian cemetery named for Louis XIV's confessor.

Périgord (**pay** ree gohr) a region in southwestern France noted for its truffles and goose livers.

Pont-Neuf (po^n **nuhf**) "new bridge"; a bridge over the Seine in Paris built, despite its name, in 1607. *Se porter comme le Pont-Neuf* is idiomatic for "to hold up like the

Pont-Neuf," that is, to be strong and healthy at an advanced age.

Provence (proh **vah^n^s**) a region of southeastern France bordering on the Mediterranean Sea and known for its ancient ruins and distinctive cuisine.

Quai d'Orsay (**kay** dohr **say**) the site of the French Foreign Ministry in Paris, and hence the Foreign Ministry itself.

Reims/Rheims (ra^n^) an industrial city in northeastern France with vast wine-producing and storage facilities (especially champagne), a notable Gothic cathedral, and an unpronounceable name.

> I would ask English-speaking visitors to the cathedral town of **Rheims** to stop trying to pronounce the town's name correctly—that is, trying to make it sound like something between a clearing of the throat and a sinus attack. As we all know, the French have a special organ in their noses that makes such pronunciations effortless, but very few English-speakers are so equipped. Speakers of English should therefore do what comes naturally, and in a loud voice always refer to **Rheims** as "Reems."
>
> —CULLEN MURPHY, *The Atlantic*

Rive Gauche (reev **gohsh**) the Left Bank of the Seine in Paris, traditionally the center of French student and artistic life.

Rolland Garros (roh **lah^n^** gah **roh**) the tennis stadium in Paris where the French Open is played.

Sacré-Coeur (**sah** kray **kuhr**) a church atop Montmartre with commanding views of Paris.

Saint Cyr (sa^n^ **seer**) the French national military academy, in the town of the same name in northern France.

Saint-Tropez (**sa^n^** troh **pay**) a popular seaside resort in the southeast of France.

(la) Sorbonne ([lah] sohr **bun**) France's most famous university, founded in 1253 and located in Paris.

Tuileries (tweel **ree**) public gardens in Paris located between the Louvre and the Place de la Concorde.

Vergeze (vehr **zhez**) the place near Arles in southern France where a naturally carbonated water bubbles to the surface and is marketed worldwide as Perrier.

Versailles (vehr **sai**) a city in northern France famous both for its palace, built by successive French kings on the site of the hunting lodge of Louis XIII, and as the place where the treaty ending World War I was signed in 1919.

Vichy (**vee** shee) the seat of the French collaborationist government during World War II, and thus a synonym for collaboration with an enemy.

Index

〰